Inventor 2013

Bearing house

Frede Uhrskov

Foreword

This booklet is an update and rewrites the same book to Release 5, 5.3, 6, 8, 9, 10, 11, 2008 2009, 2010 and 2012.

Since there is a wide range of changes in the structure of the subject, will the booklets in teaching contexts could not be used concurrently.

Images for this book is downloaded when the program has been installed under Windows 7 It can sometimes cause a slight difference in appearance to the screen as you work with.

The booklet is intended for beginners, which in a simple and straightforward way to be introduced to the program.
It thus requires no previous knowledge of the program to use the booklet. For many courses, I have found strengths and weaknesses in the material, therefore, been attempted is made even more user friendly and accurate.

I hope you enjoy the book.

Holsted 2012

Frede Uhrskov

Table of Contents

Presentations

In this exercise we will construct a casting, a pillow block bearing for a shaft. The bed looks like and has the dimensions shown:

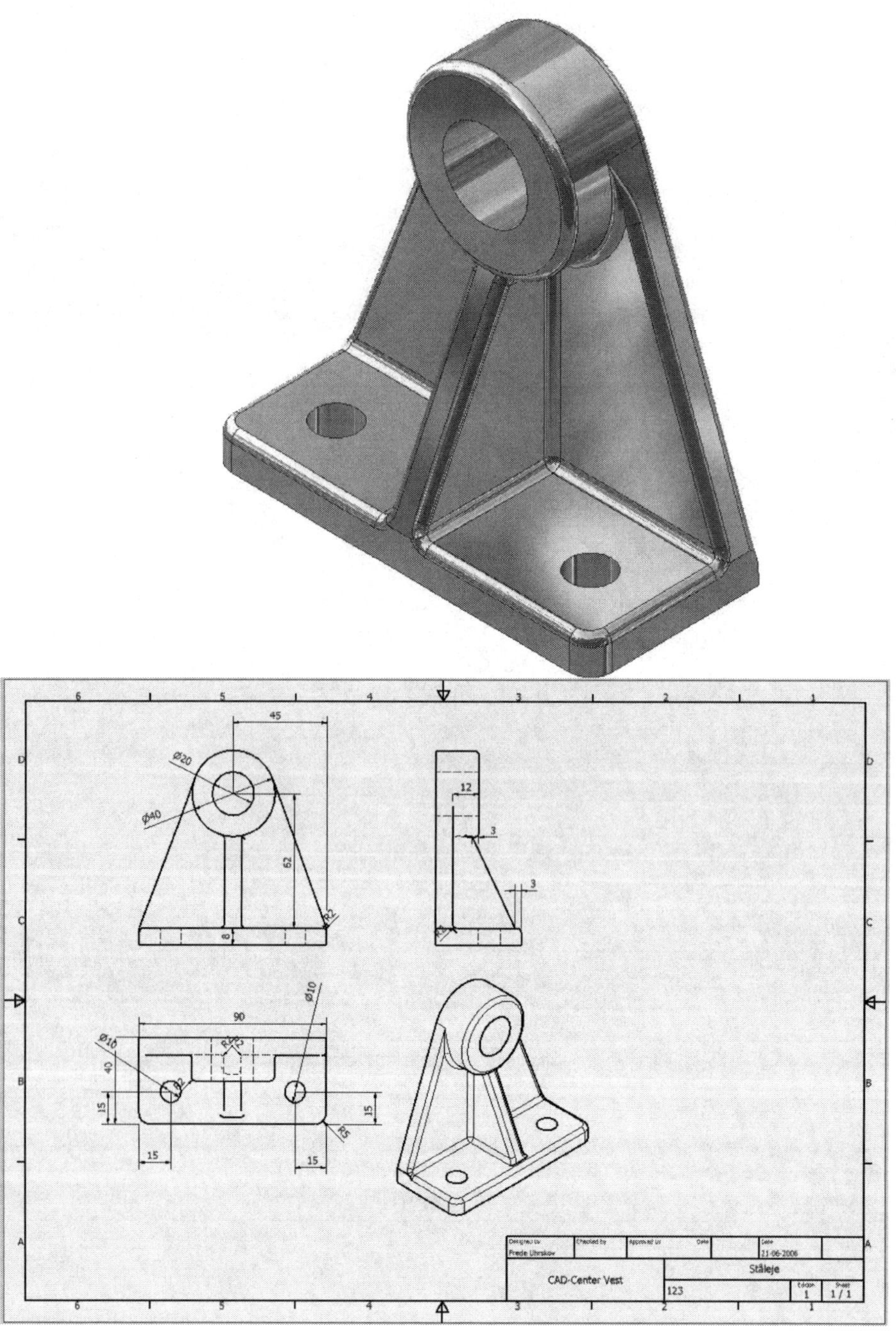

Templates

The Inventor is working with various templates that are related to the task being per-
formed.
The various templates have such uses.

Sheet Metal.ipt is used when you need to create threads of plates to be
bend and when you must make unfolding.

Standard.iam is used when you should make assemblies of the indi-
vidual parts, which has been constructed.

Standard.idw is used when you should make drawings of the individ-
ual parts.

Standard.ipn is used when you should make en Presentation of a simple part or en assembly.

Standard.ipt is used when you have to construct the topics as the
structure will consist of. It can be molded, turned or machined parts.

Weldment.iam is used when one needs to show welds in an assembly.

Standard.dwg makes it possible to create an Inventor part from an
AutoCAD drawing. You can create your own Inventor template from
an existing AutoCAD drawing - look in the help file for more information.

One must know in advance what kind of a drawing or design that you need to start with.
Then choose the appropriate template.

Inventor 2013

When you enter the program, there will be a start-up screen as shown:

Draw area is empty and you must start by creating a part or project, but in this case we will go directly to produce a part.

Click **New**

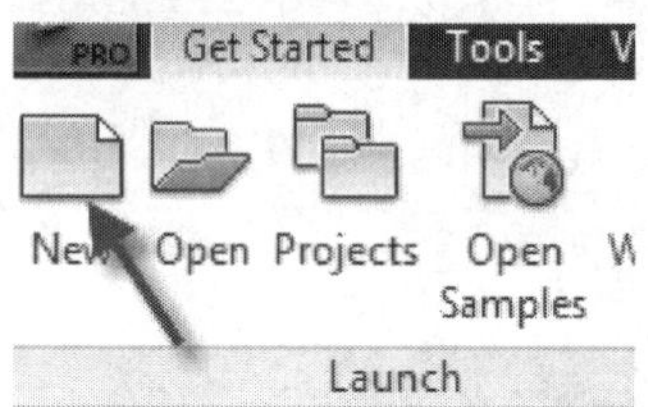

Copyright © 2012 Frede Uhrskov

This opens a new dialog where you can choose which file type you want to open.

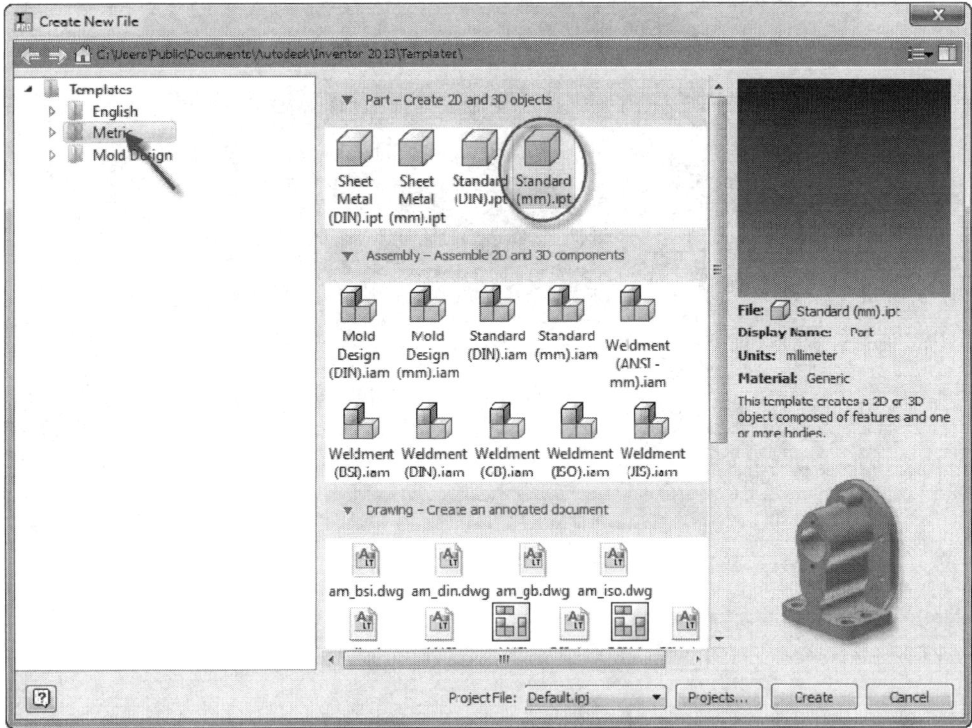

If you have made your setup right, the displayed items would be default.

You can now create your part by clicking **Create**

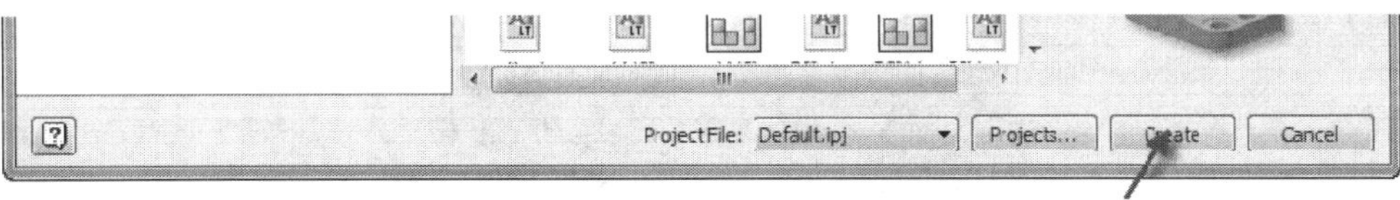

A new part is created - called **Partx**

A new part

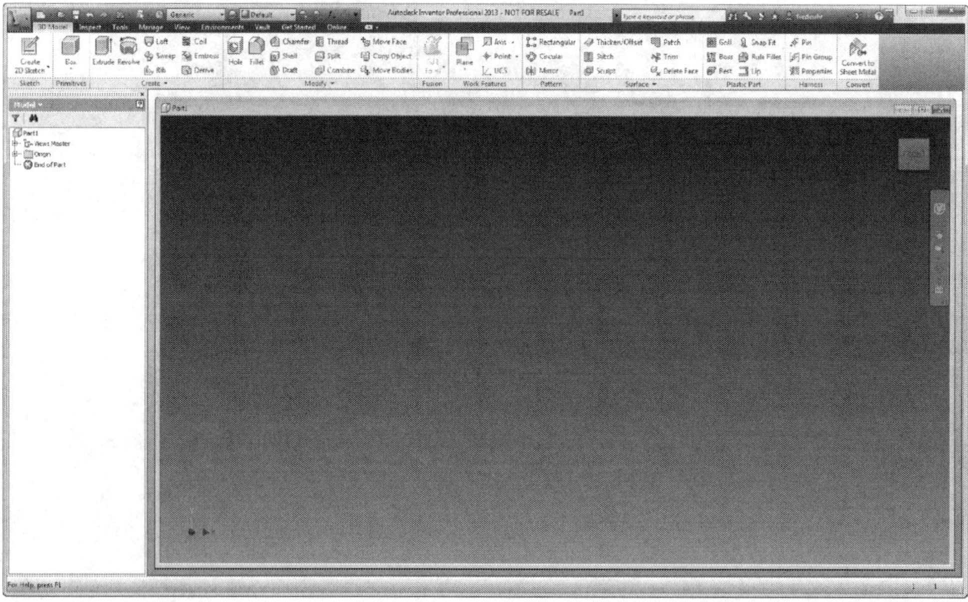

Start clicking **Create 2D Sketch**

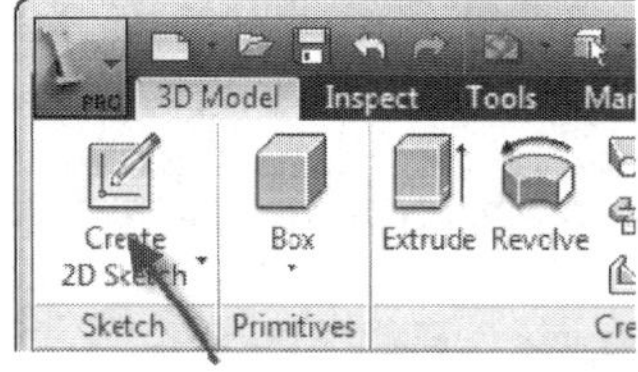

The screen changes and you must choose the plan that you want to sign in.

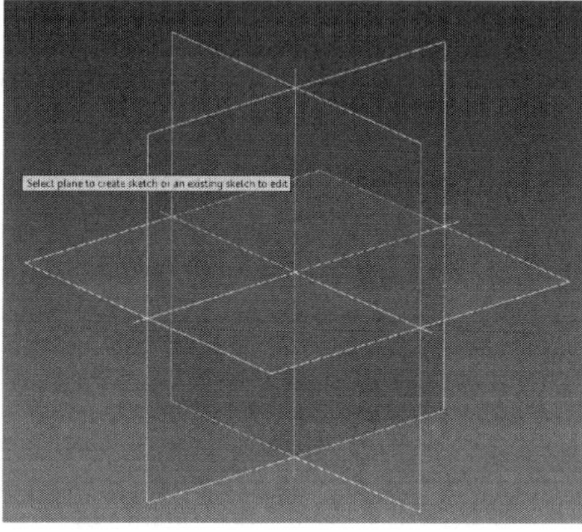

Select the XY plane as shown on next page

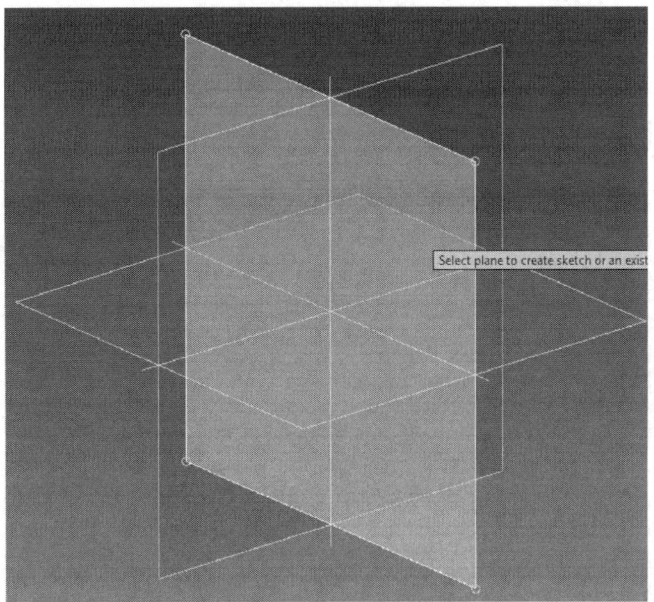

The plan change so you have the origin in the middle of the screen and XY axes lie in a normal coordinate system.

Rectangle

Draw a rectangle starting from 0.0 and the objectives 90 x 40. You can change the input field with the Tab key.

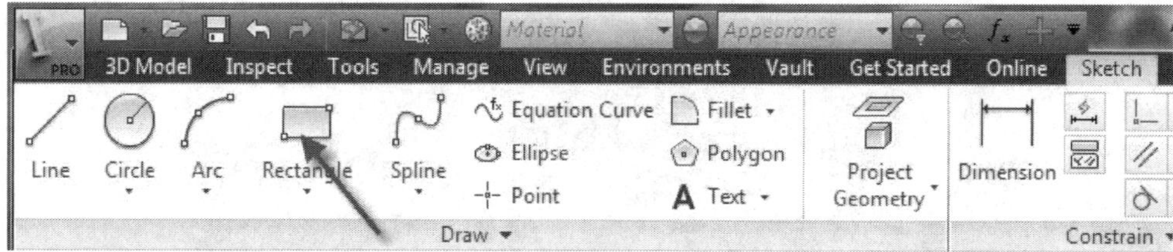

Right click and select **Finish 2D Sketch**

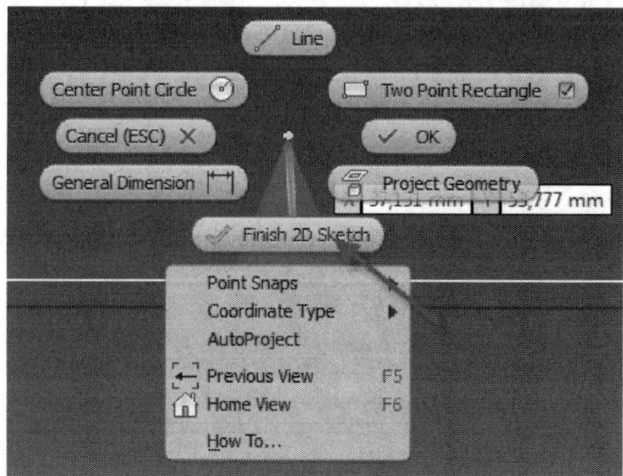

Isometric view

Press **F6** to get an isometric view - try to learn the shortcut keys, as it can save much time and lessen your burden on the mouse hand.

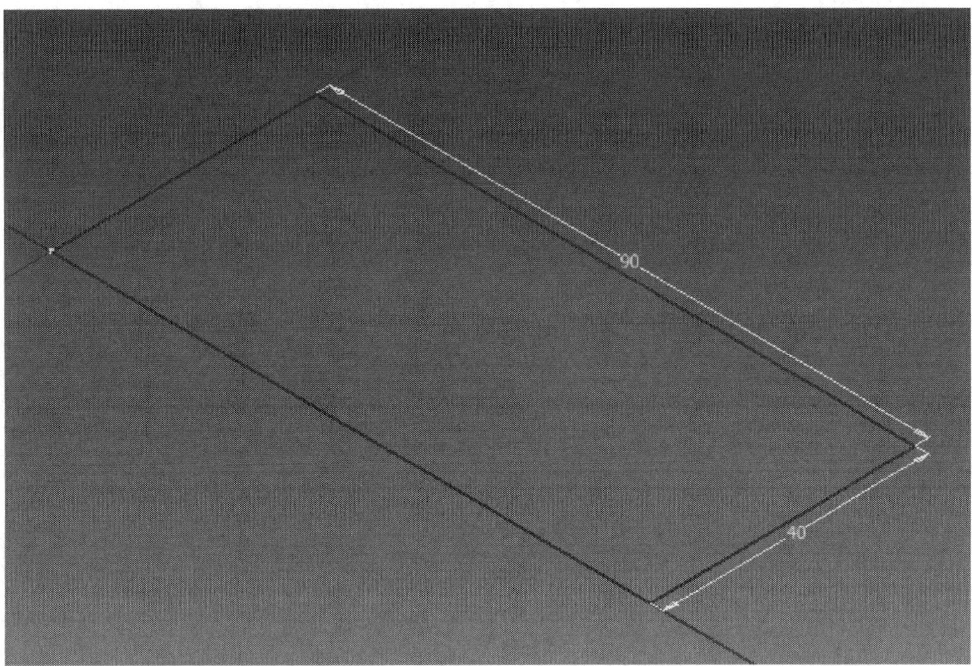

Click **Finish Sketch** - the ribbon changes to **Model**

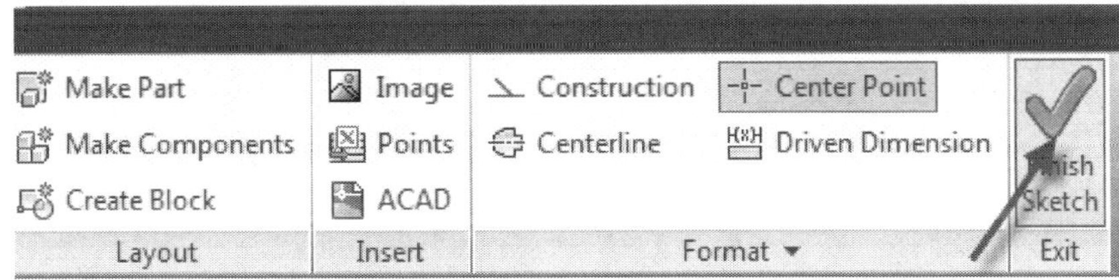

Extrude

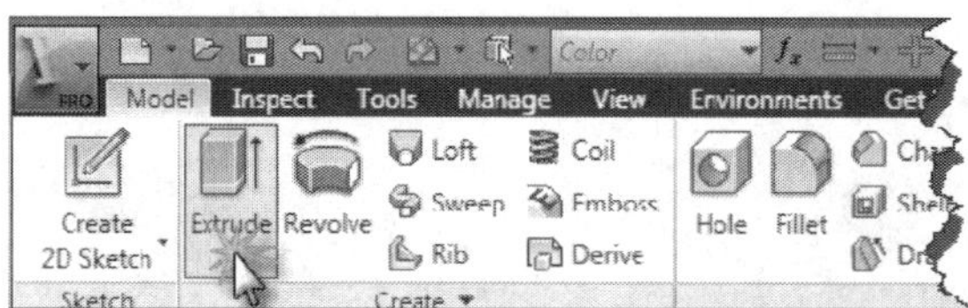

Choose **Extrude**

Now you can see the rectangle as a **Profile** and the size of the 3-dimensional figure on the screen.

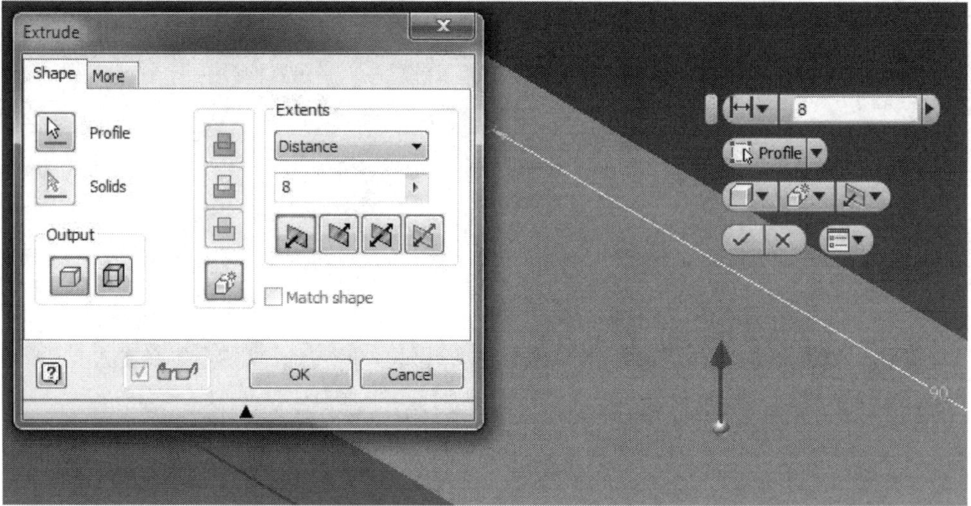

In the dialog box, select the extrusion direction:

In the **Extents** selected function **Distance** and extrusion size to **8**

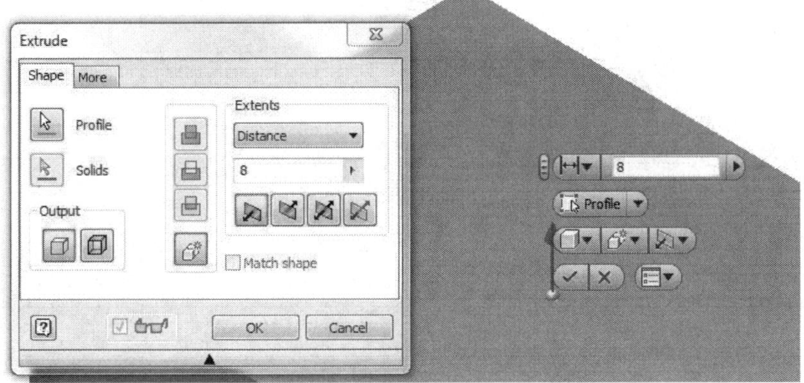

Note the figures to the right - they show, among other things the extrusion direction.

Click **OK**

The various features of the extrusion can also be selected in the small icons that are displayed on the object itself.

Now the figure looks like this:

New Sketch

We now have created a new sketch, and it must be on the farthest long vertical surface.

Right click and select **New Sketch**

Move the cursor to the rear of the surface - hold still for a moment - until the text **1. Face** shows up:

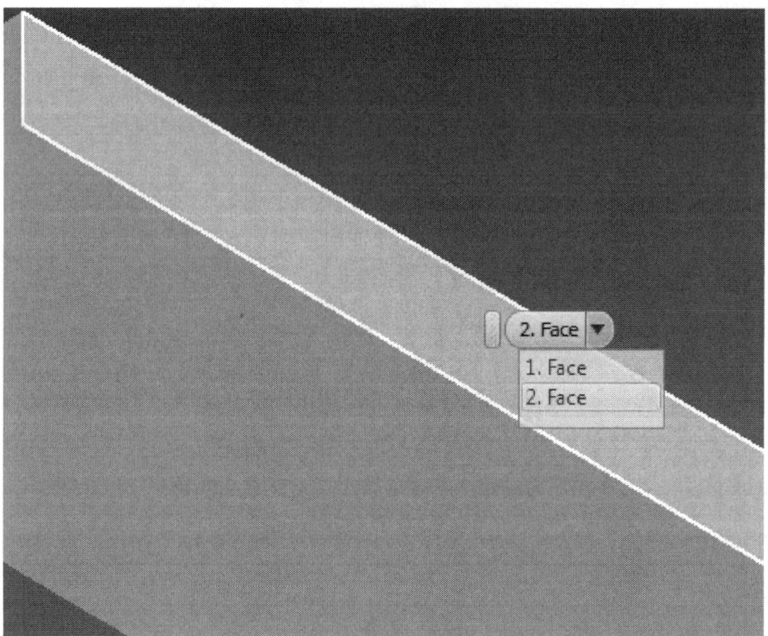

Choose **2. Face**

Inventor is now automatically shape so you look perpendicularly onto the selected surface.

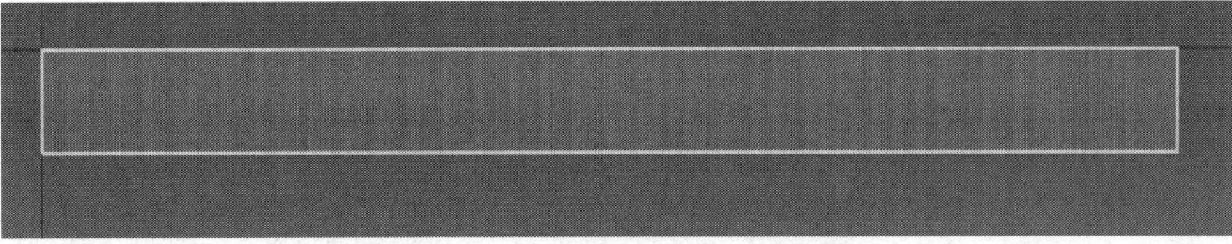

Unfortunately, the figure comes Inventor "wrong" when it comes to lie in fourth quadrant and coordinate turns and inappropriate.

Click twice on the rotation arrow in **View Cube**

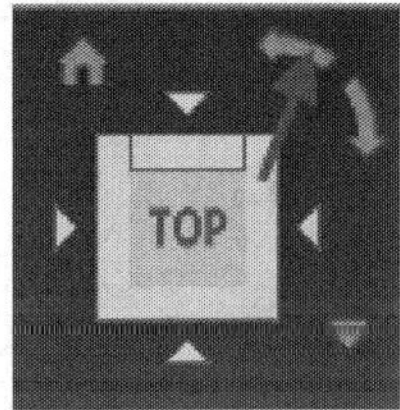

Now we have the topic we want.

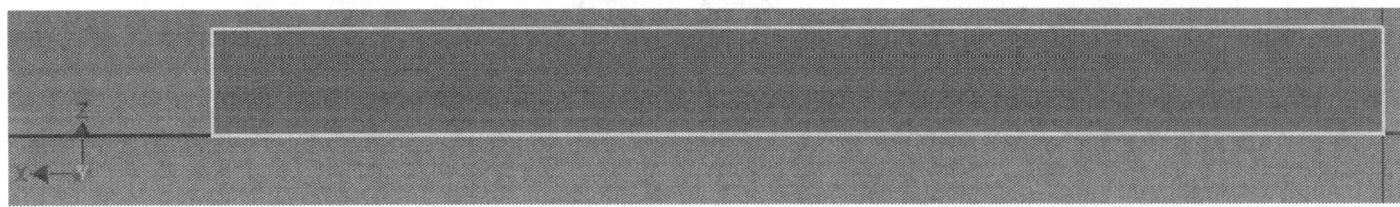

The panel has now shifted to Sketch with all design tools.

We must now start to draw a circle to be placed above the center of the figure.

Select the Circle command

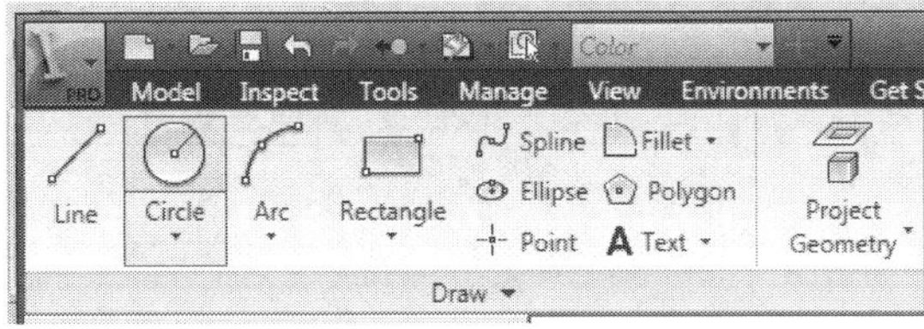

Move the cursor over the top line until it snaps to the midpoint of the line - you can see this by the cursor changes color.

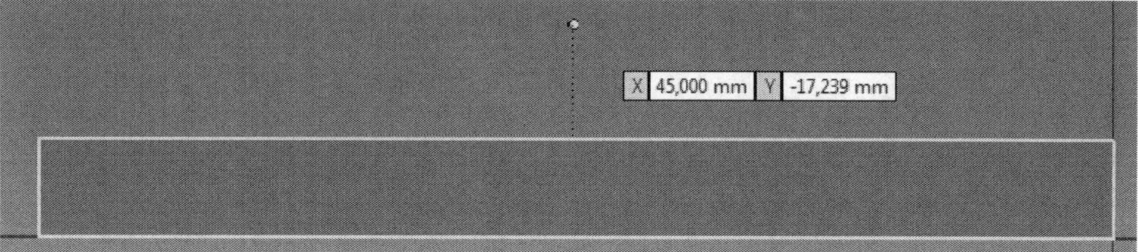

Now pull straight up - there comes a thin dotted line that shows that you drag vertically - note that the Y value is negative.

Change input field with the Tab key and enter -62.

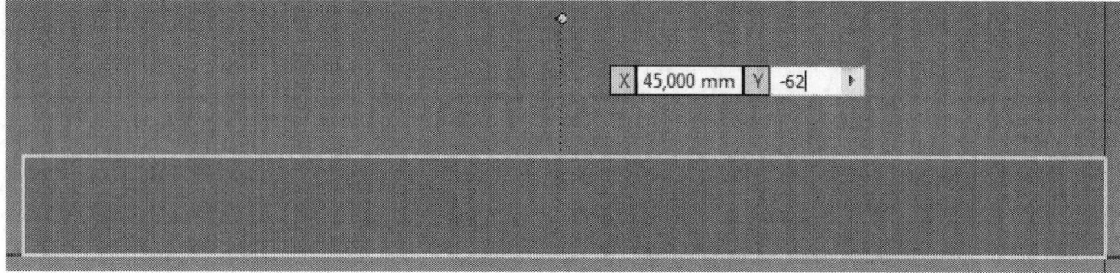

Enter the circle's diameter to 40

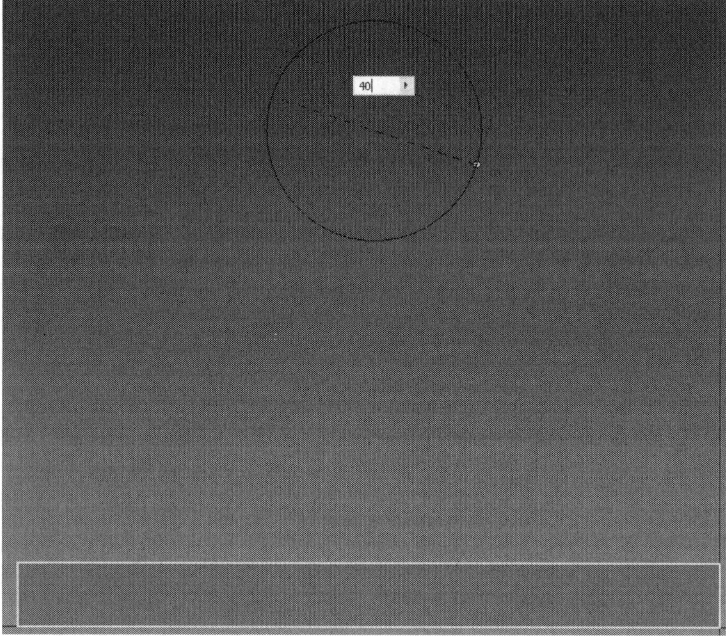

Select **Line**

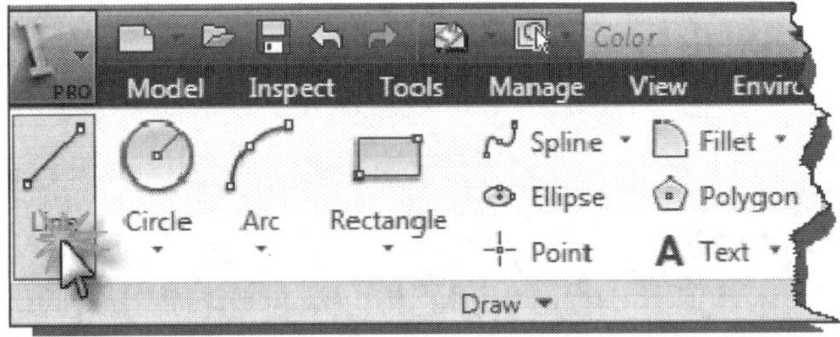

Now drag a line from the edge of the block and to the circle - it should snap to the tangent point, which automatically occurs:

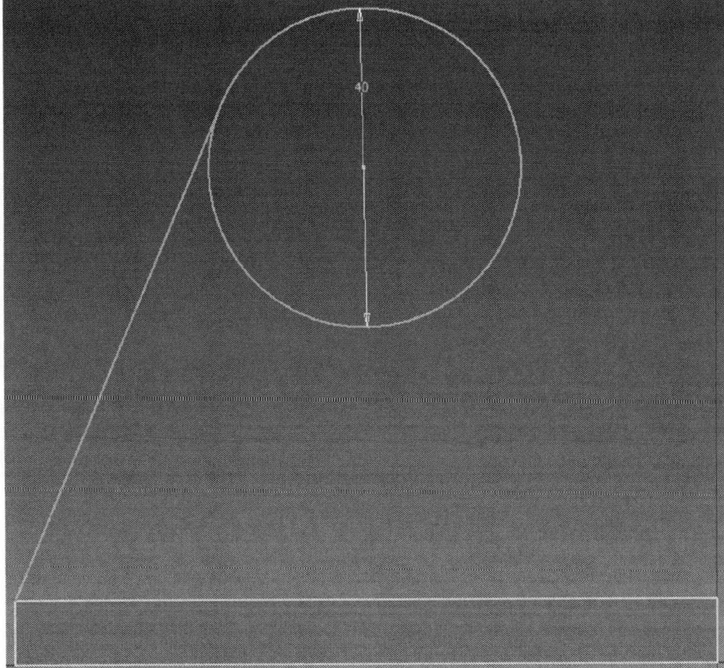

Draw a similar line in the opposite side.

Hit the **F6** to see the figure in isometric.

Trim

Now the lower section of the circle shall be removed:

Choose **Trim** in 2D Sketch Panel

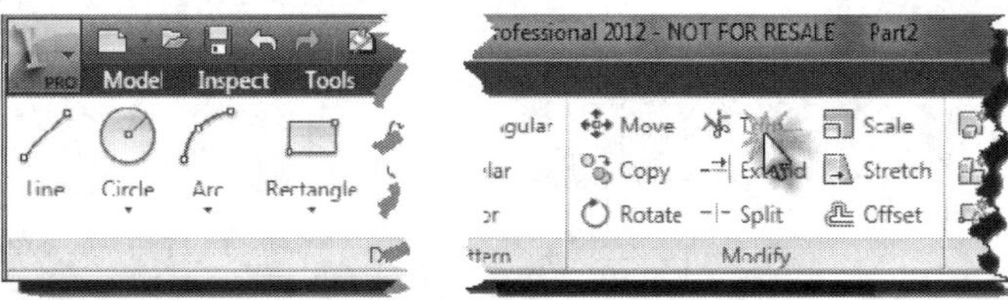

Move the cursor to the bottom of the circle - click on the line. The line disappears and the profile is completed:

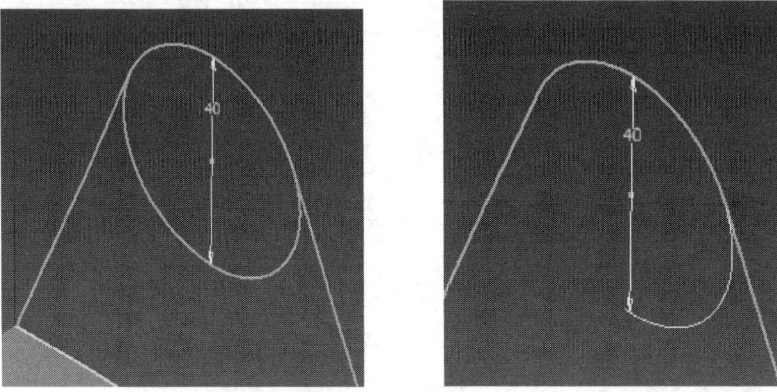

Right click and select **Finish 2D Sketch**

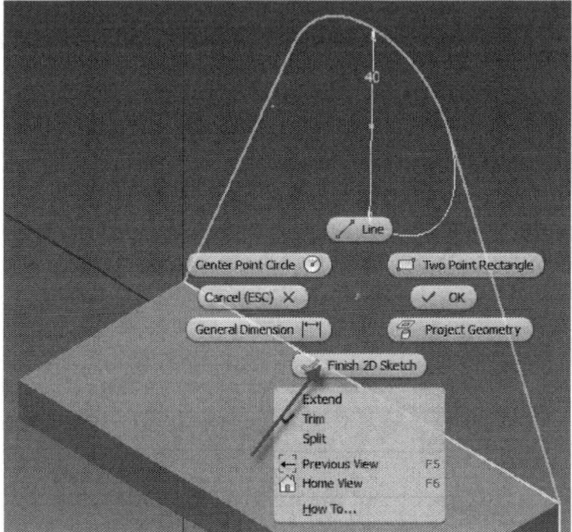

Extrude

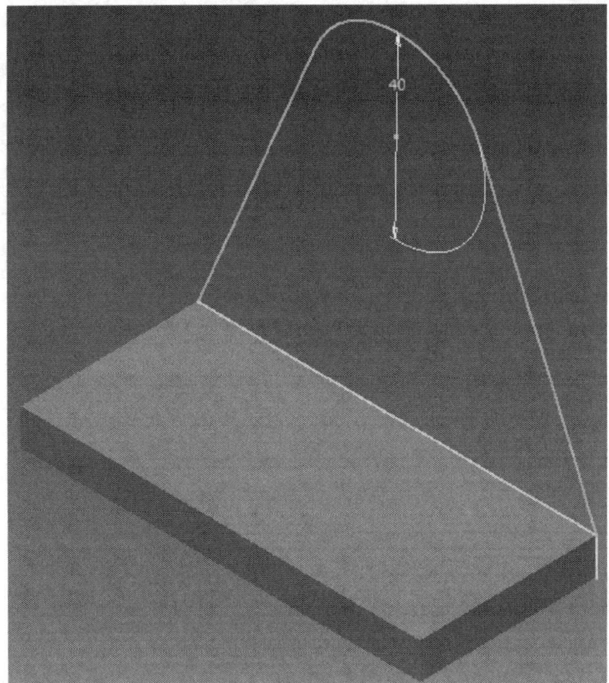

Choose **Extrude**

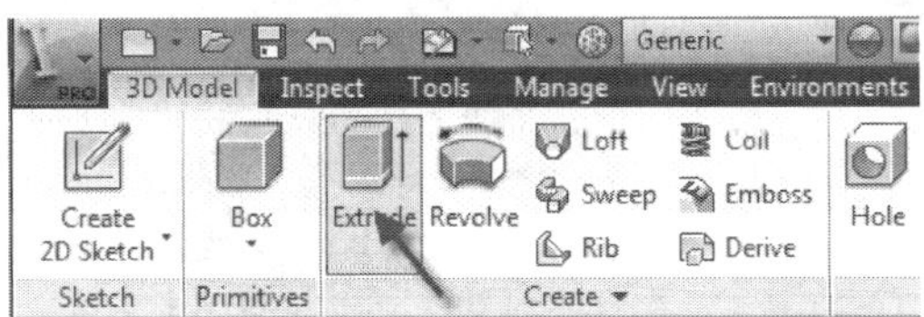

Click the profile we just created

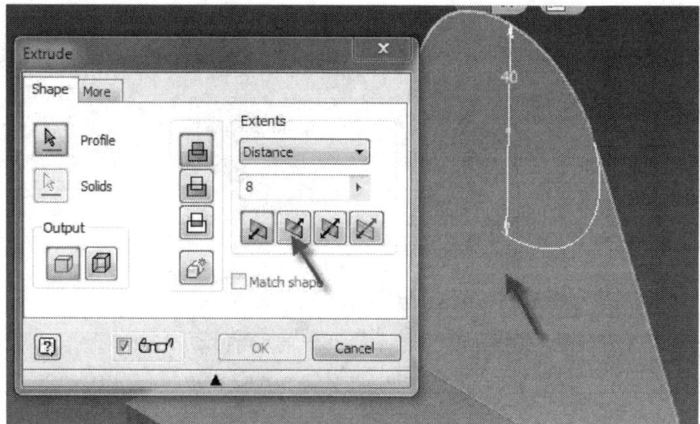

The profile is highlighted and is ready to be extruded

Choose direction and enter the value **8** in the input field.

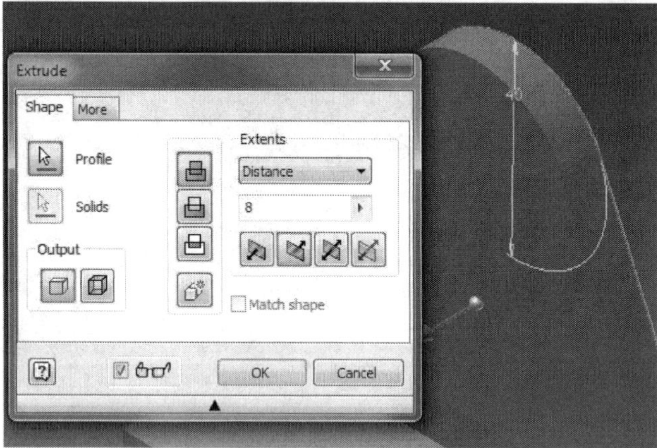

Click **OK**

The bearing house will now look like this:

Right click and choose **New Sketch**

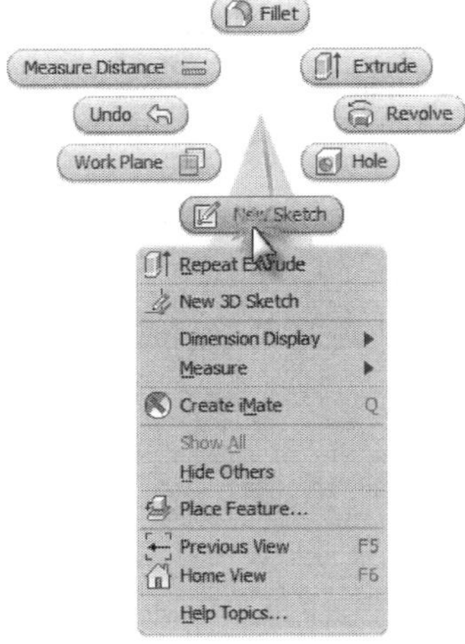

Click on the near face of the vertical profile

Inventor turns the figure and you look at the designated area.

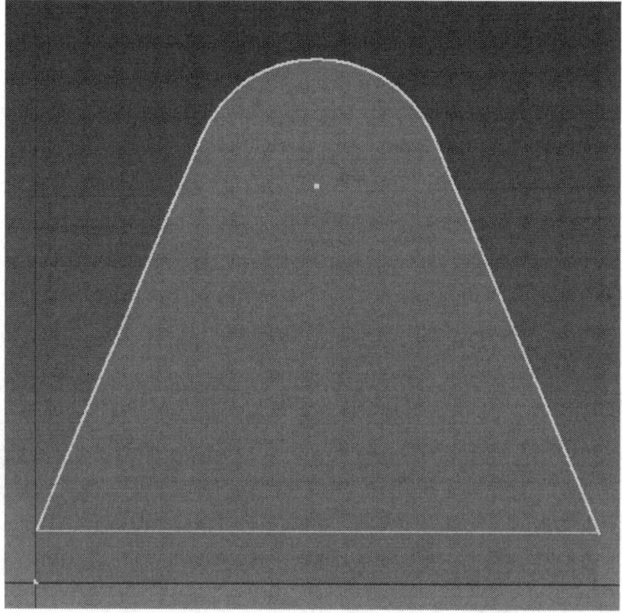

Now draw a circle concentric with the upper arc and the periphery framework of the existing arc - note that it will snap to the arc.

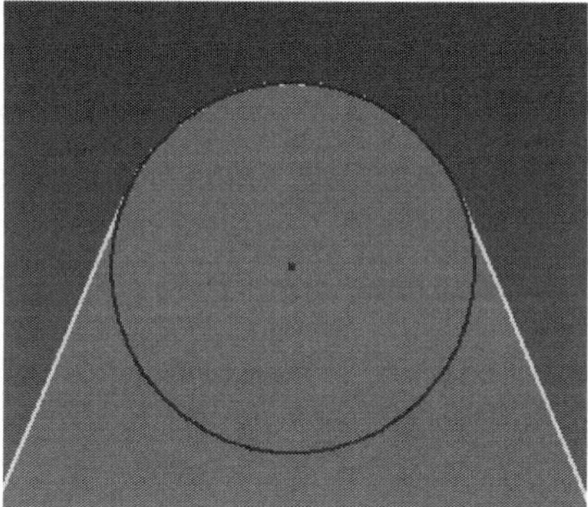

Right click and choose **Finish 2D Sketch**

Right click og choose **Extrude**

Choose **Join**

Designate the circle as **Profile** and paste extrusion to **12**

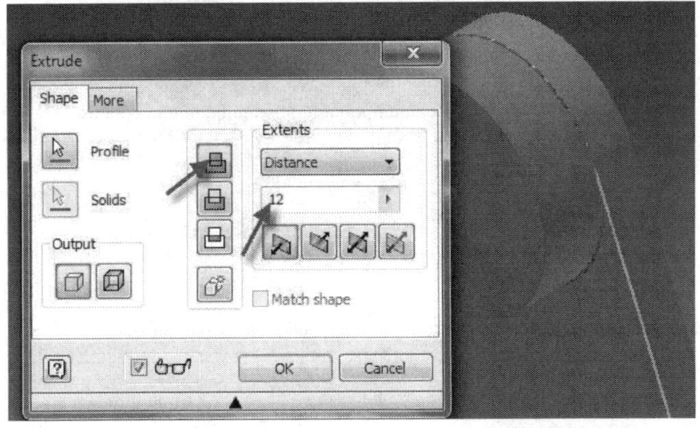

Click **OK**

Right click og choose **New Sketch**

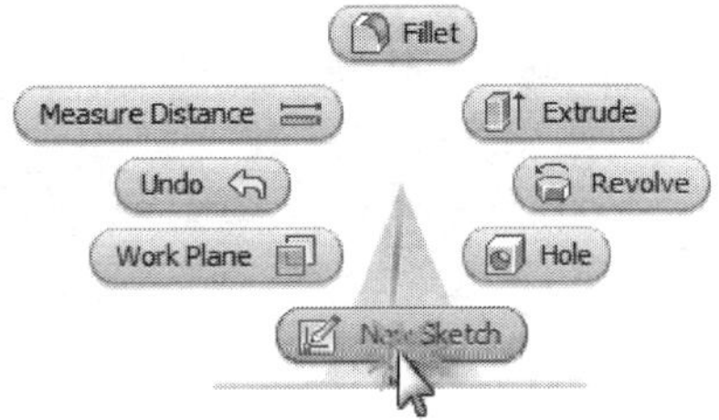

Click on the nearest surface of the round profile.

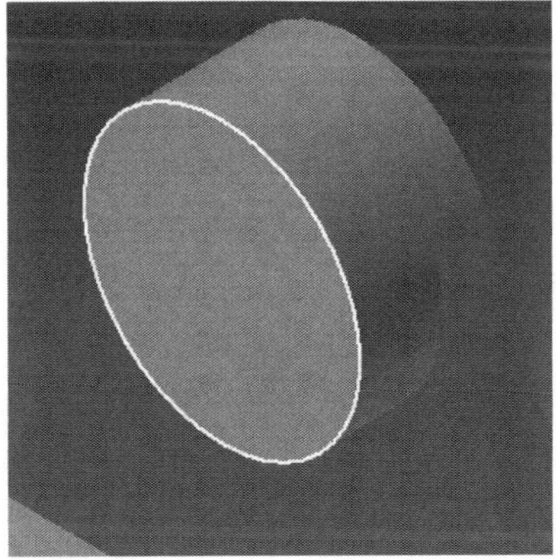

The figure turns the face to you - and that makes it easy to draw a concentric circle.

Now draw a circle whose center is already established center with a diameter of 20

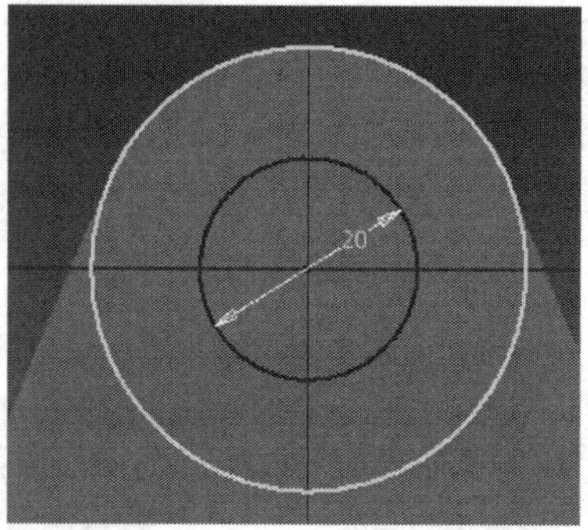

Right click - Choose **Finish 2D Sketch**

Right click og Choose **Extrude**

Designate the circle as **Profile**

Make your choice as shown in the dialog box.

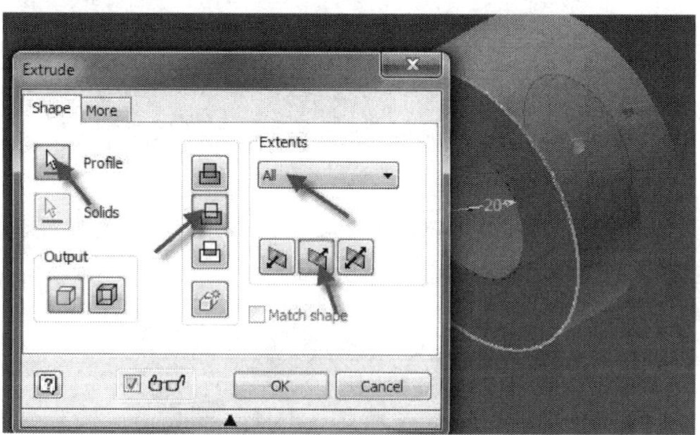

The extrusion appears

Click **OK**

Save the design

Work Plane

We must now make the stiffener in the middle of the topic and for that we need a function that creates a work plan (Work Plane) at the point where we want to work.

Right click and Choose **Work Plane**

Click on the displayed border when the cursor snaps to the midpoint

There is now an outline of the working plane.

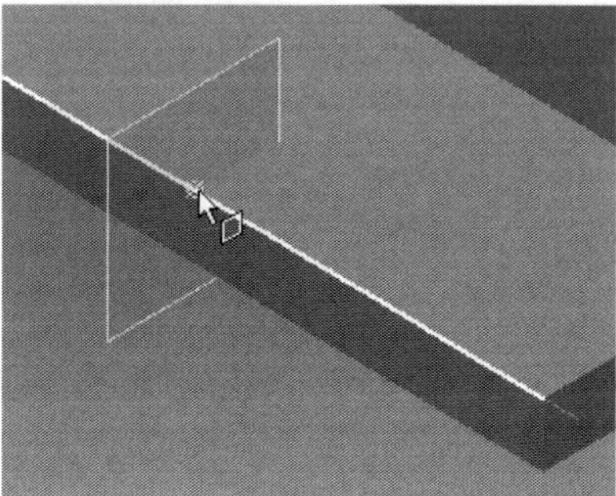

Copyright © 2012 Frede Uhrskov

Click again at the center of the edge - working plane created:

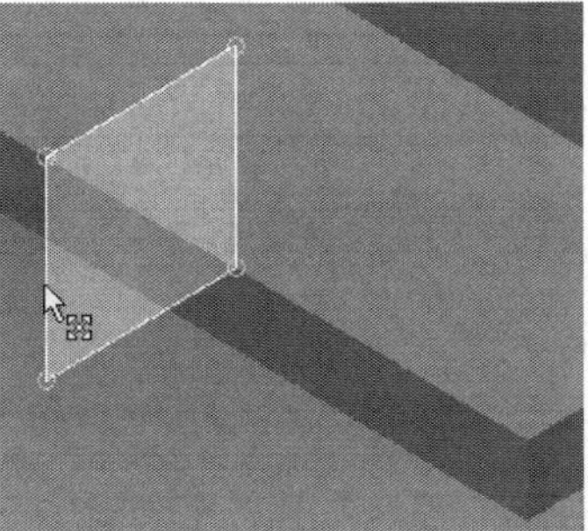

Click on the little figure as shown in the picture

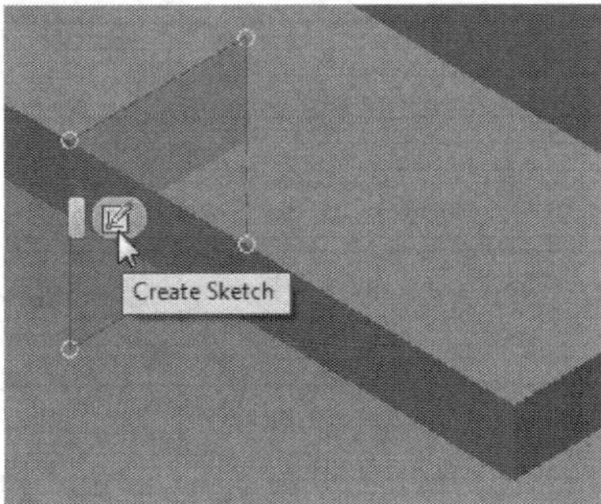

This will create a sketch plane and the image is rotated:

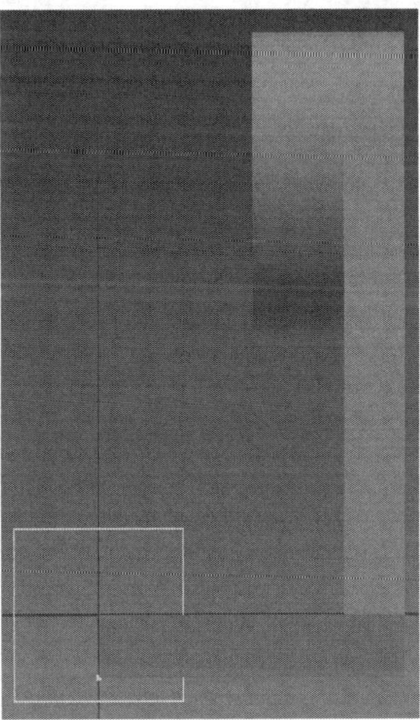

In this case, I think it is best to see the figure isometric.

Hit **F6**

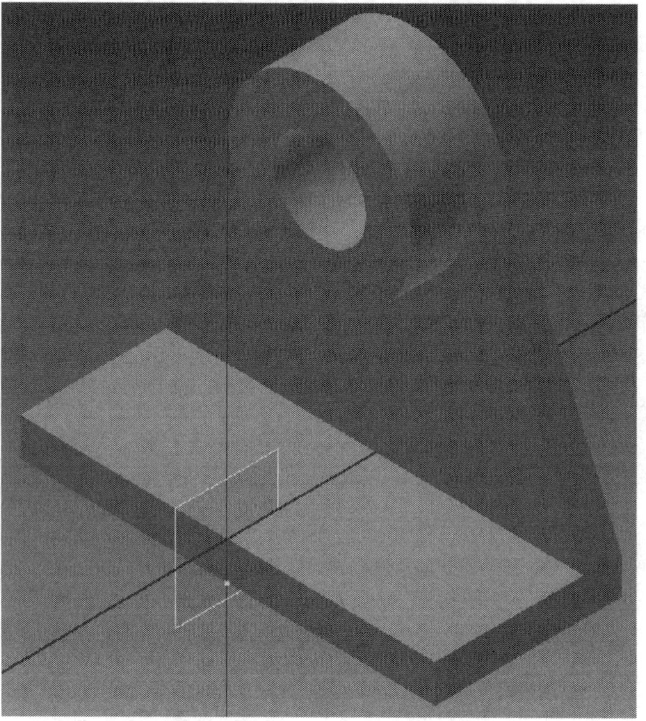

Slice Graphics

It is practical to see only half of the pedestal so we will temporarily remove the fore-most part of the subject.

Right click og choose **Slice Graphics** or hit **F7**

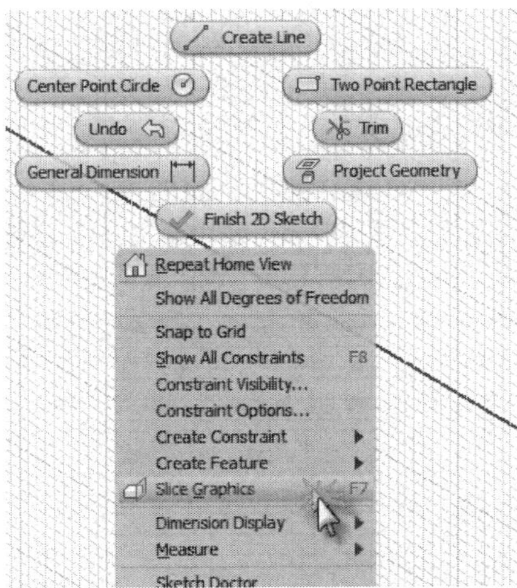

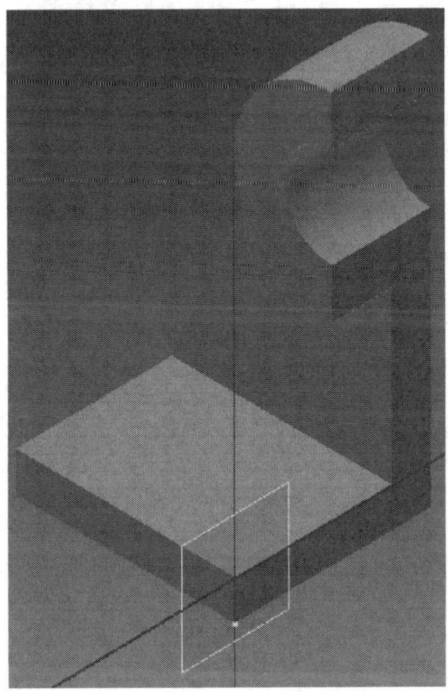

Now the front of the work piece is hidden and the working plane is free.

Project Geometry

Choose **Project Cut Edges** placed under **Project Geometry**

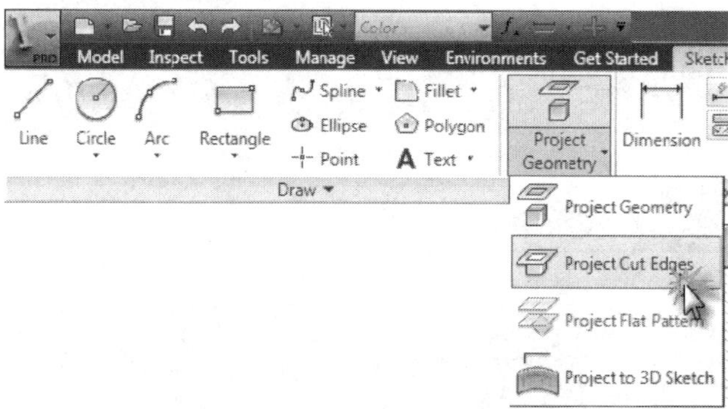

Inventor now automatically form construct lines on all edges of the cut object.

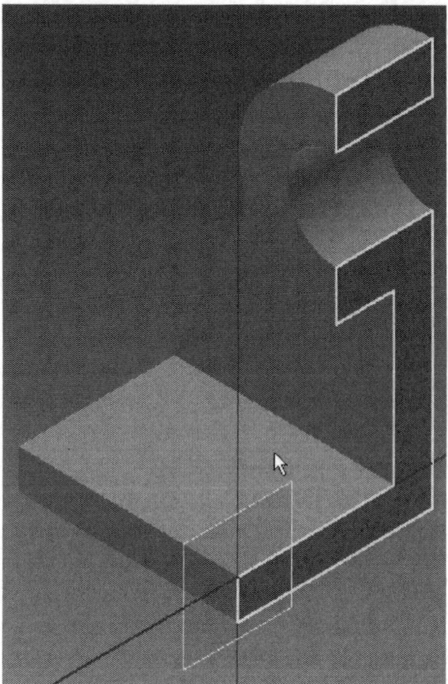

RIB

Draw a line starting 3 mm. from the upper left corner.

Note that you can enter the starting point for the line directly in the input box - use the Tab key to enter the field.

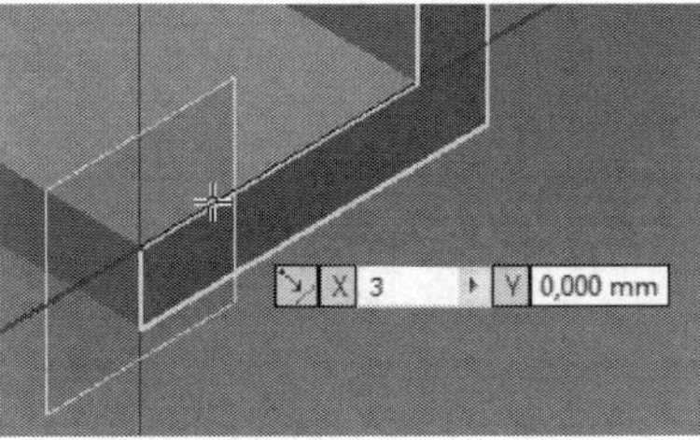

Now drag the line to the top edge as shown below:

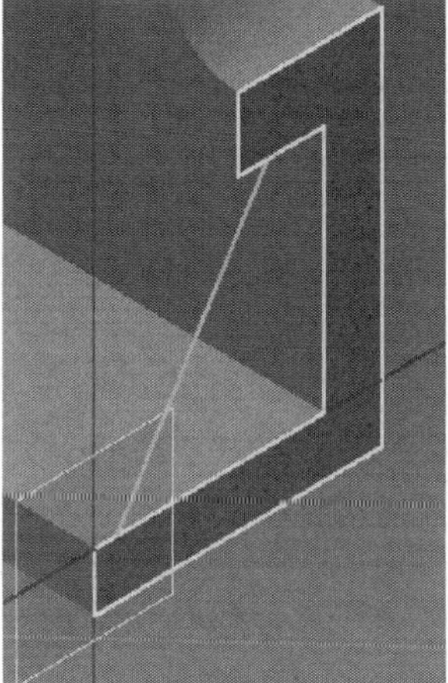

Let the line hit a random spot on the line - to get the right location, you must create a dimension that indicates the distance from the front edge to the end point of the line - look next page.

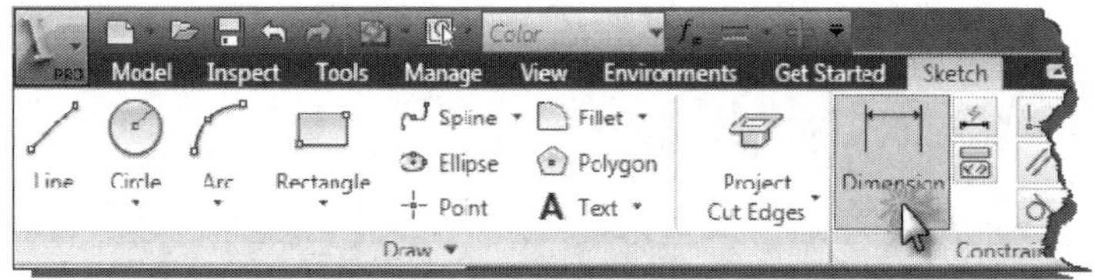

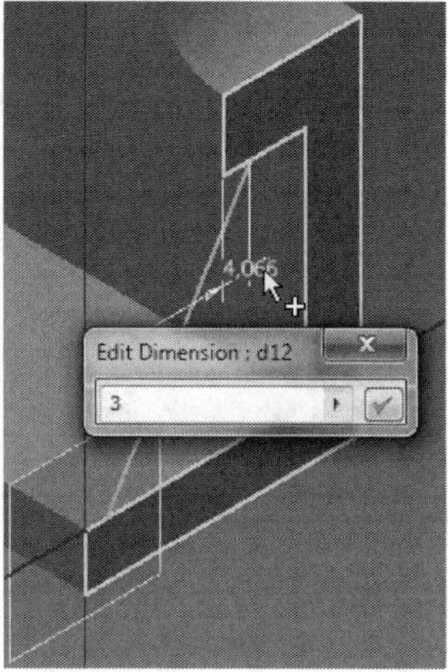

Right click and Choose **Finish 2D Sketch**

Choose **Rib**

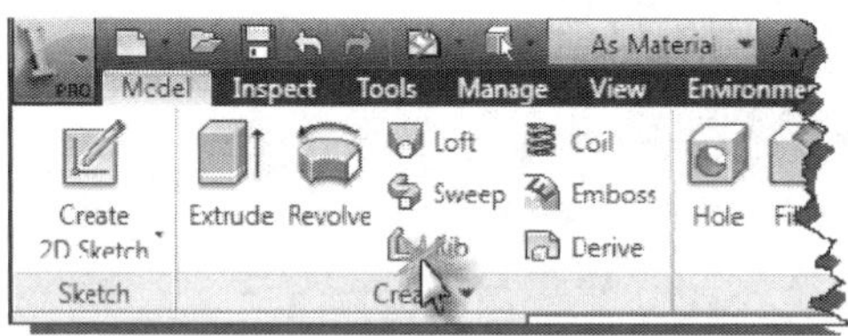

A dialog box appears and you must choose several things:

Choose **Profile** and identify the line that we drew before.

Choose the shown field and set **Thickness** to **8 mm.**

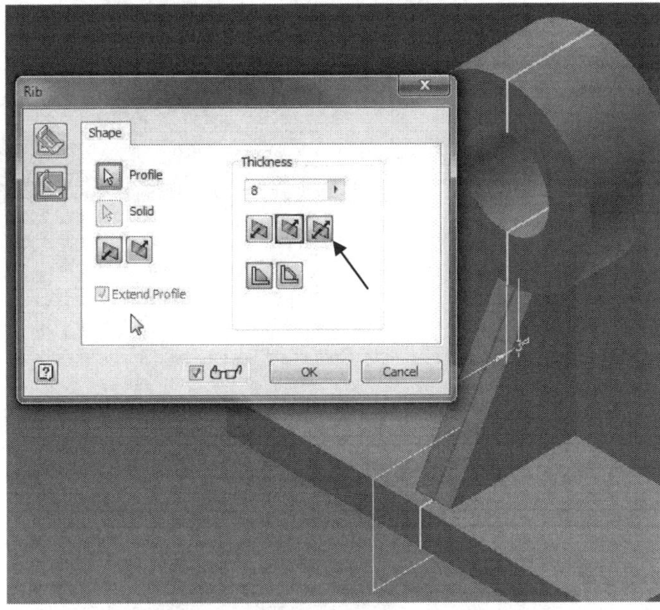

Click **OK**

Nu er ribben færdig:

Look At

One of the cleverest things by constructing a rib as shown on the previous pages, the rib adapted to the curve as it goes up against. We can easily see if we look perpendicularly into the subject.

Choose **Look At**

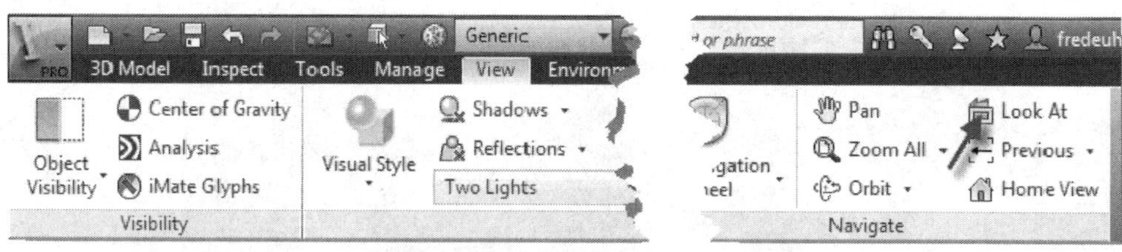

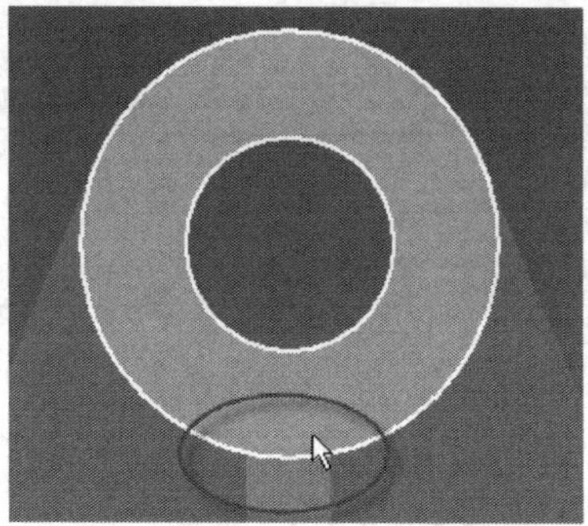

Click on the round surface facing forward - now the subject is turned and you are looking perpendicularly onto the work piece.

We can see that the rib follows the rounding.

Turn off the Work Plane

In some cases, it may be desirable to turn off the work plane, which we set up to draw the ribs.

This is done by right clicking on Work Plane in the browser and then chooses Visibility

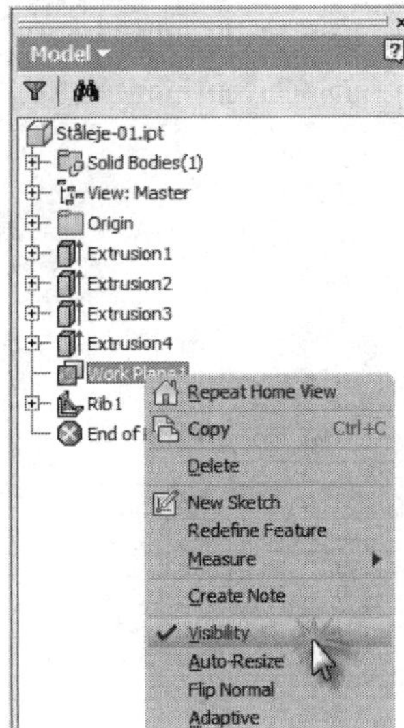

Holes

We will now make holes for attaching the pedestal - create therefore **New Sketch** on the upper horizontal surface - remember to return to the isometric view by pressing **F6**.

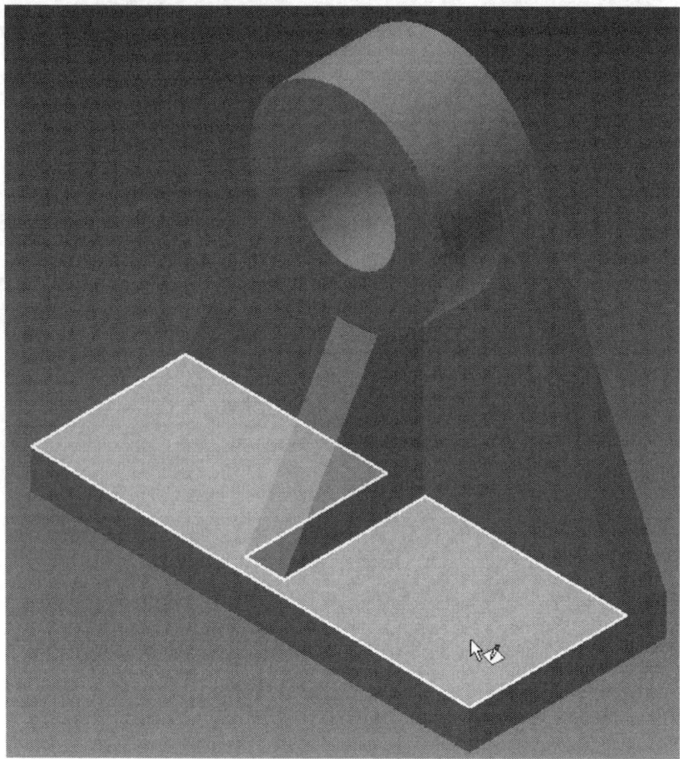

The plane is now turned perpendicular towards you:

Draw 2 circles on the planet and dimension as shown:

Hit **ESC**

Right click and choose **Finish 2D Sketch**

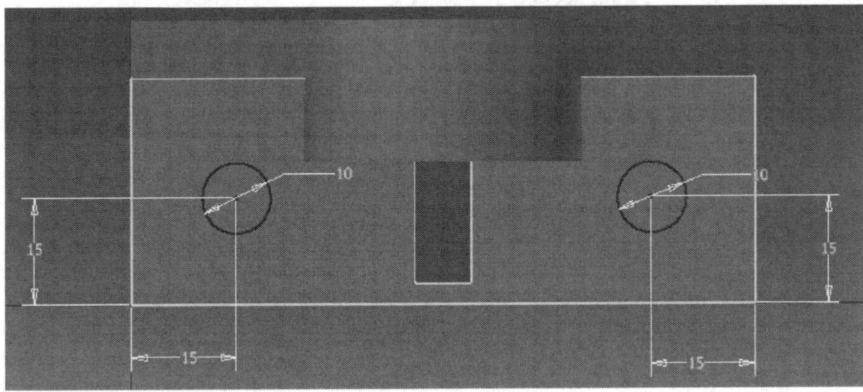

Choose **Extrude**

Choose the 2 circles as **Profiles**

Make settings as shown in the dialog box:

Click **OK**

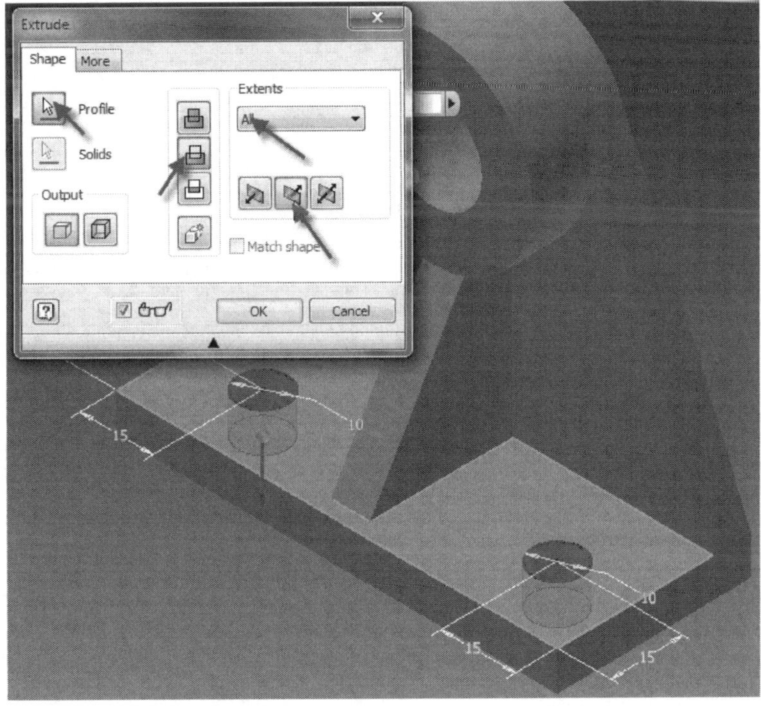

Now the bearing house looks like this:

Fillet

Right click and choose **Fillet** or hit **SHIFT+F**

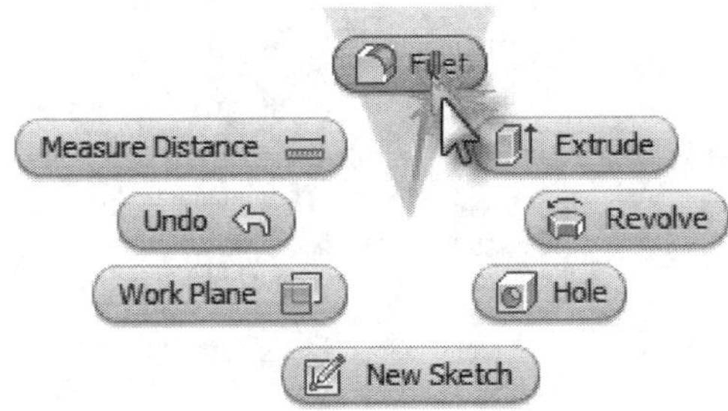

The dialog box for **Fillet** appears:

Click the two corners of the bottom surface:

Note that rounding is shown in the drawing immediately after the appointment.

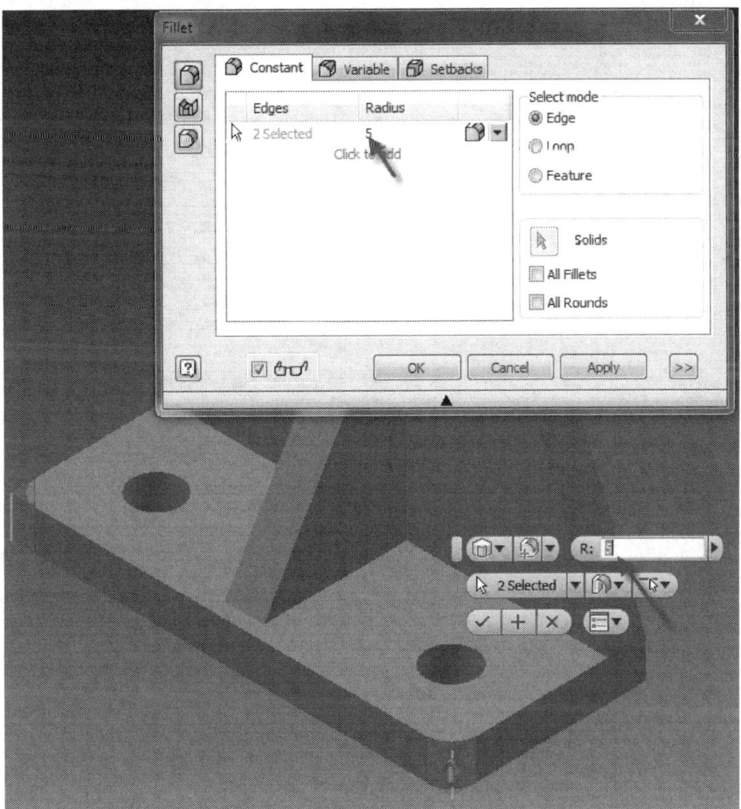

Click **OK**

Now rounding the designated corners:

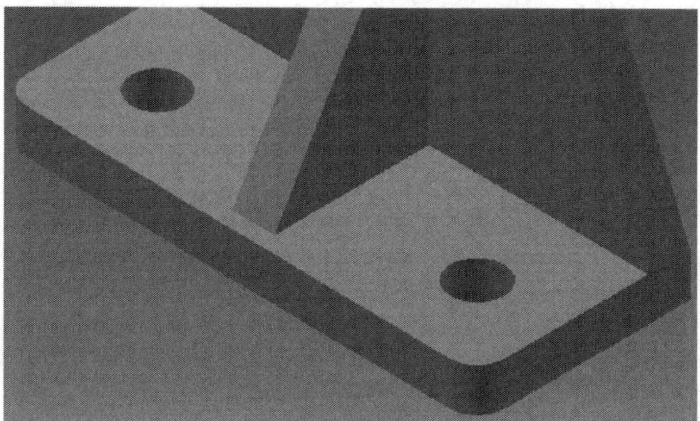

The last thing to do is rounding the edges of the bearing house.

Choose **Fillet** - set radius to 2

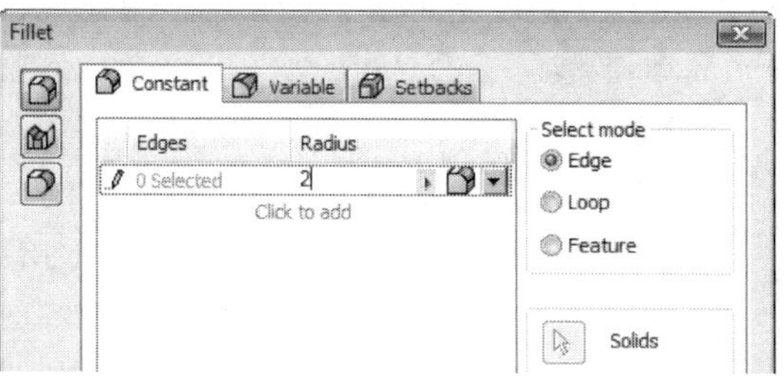

Identify the edges as you want rounded - it could be as shown below:

You can rotate the item by clicking on the corners of the cube in the upper right corner.

- Try it by yourself.

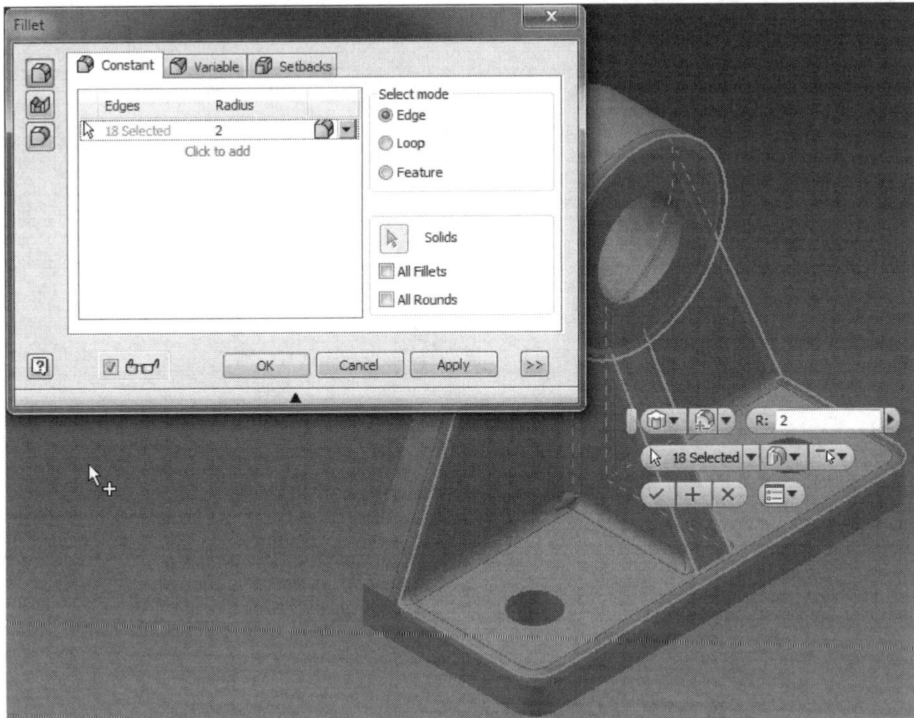

Click **OK**

Material

Try to put material on the subject by pulling down the drop menu:

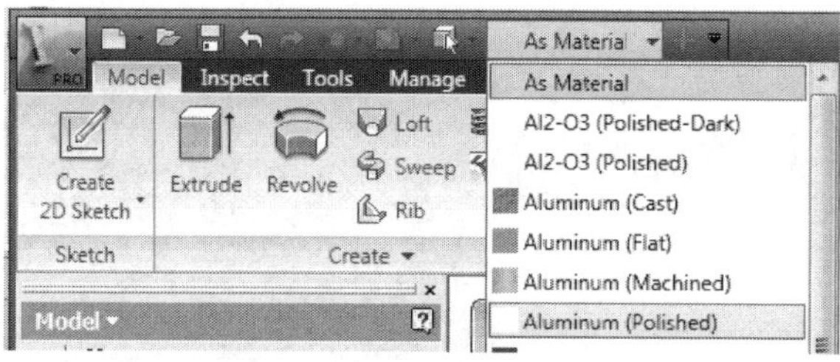

Try for example to assign material Chrome to the topic:

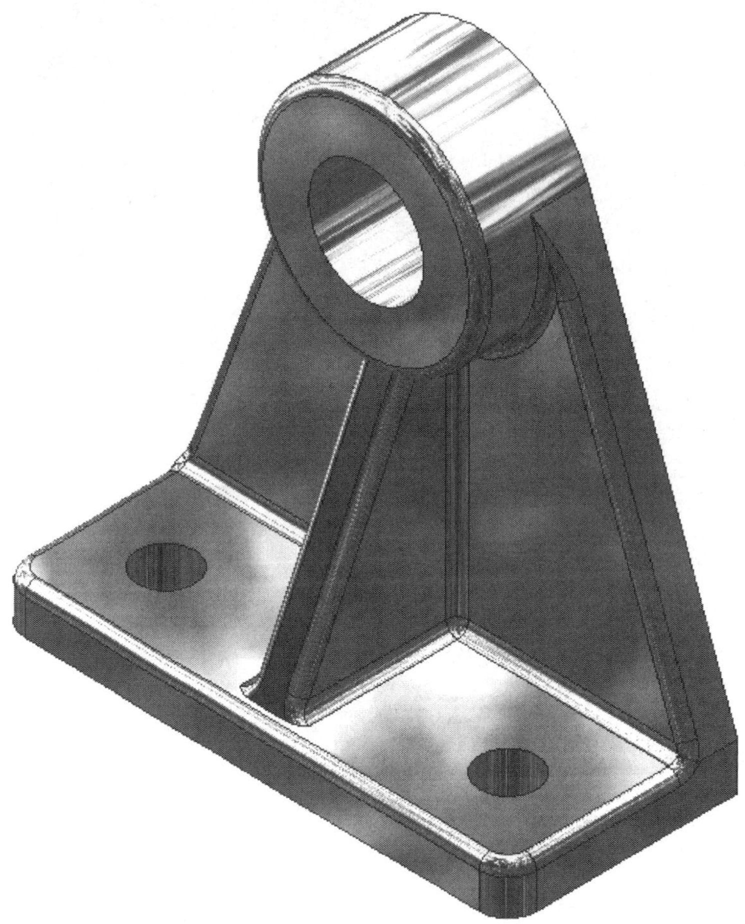

Drawings

It is now time to make drawings of the model.

For this, we must open an entirely new basic drawing:

Choose **New** and **ISO.idw**.

Click **Create**.

When you enter the Inventor, the screen should look like:

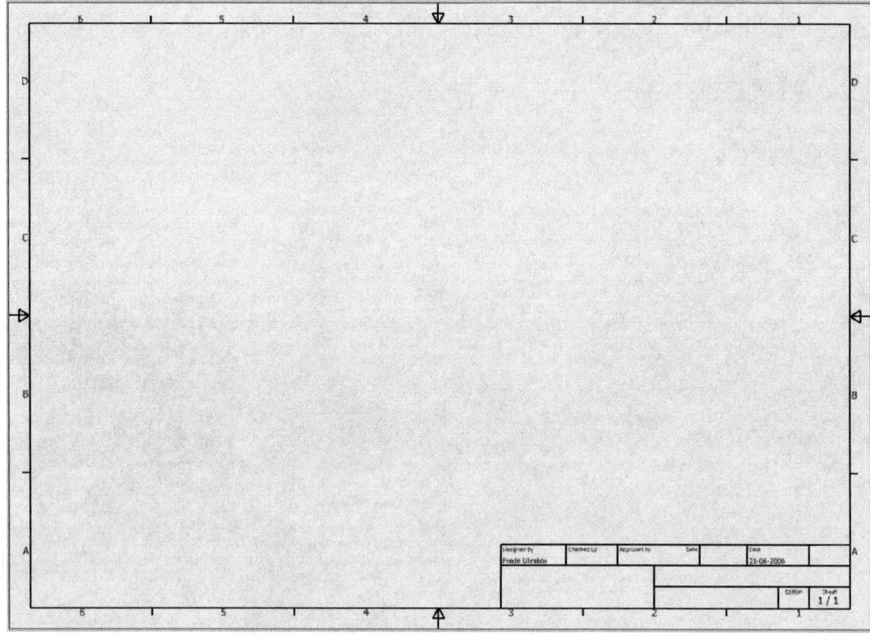

The illustrated paper with a drawing frame is a piece of A3 paper with a drawing head that contains attributes for entering information.

The drawing stamp and drawing frame can be customized, but it lies outside the boundaries of this book and will not be reviewed in this context..

Information in drawing stamp

To enter information in the drawing stamp you can either right click box **Drawing** and choose the field in **Properties**

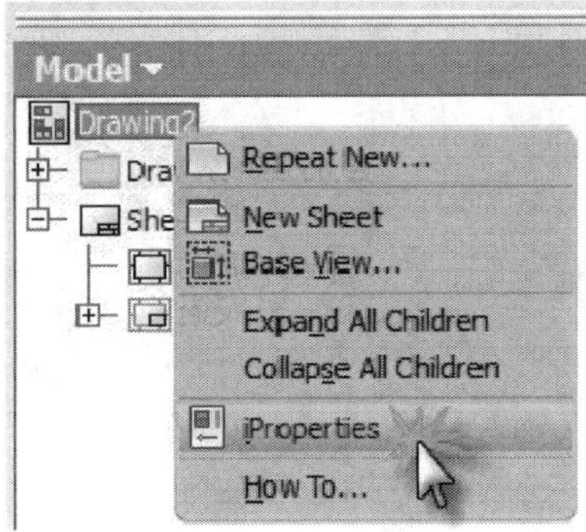

or through the Applications menu and choose the field **iProperties**

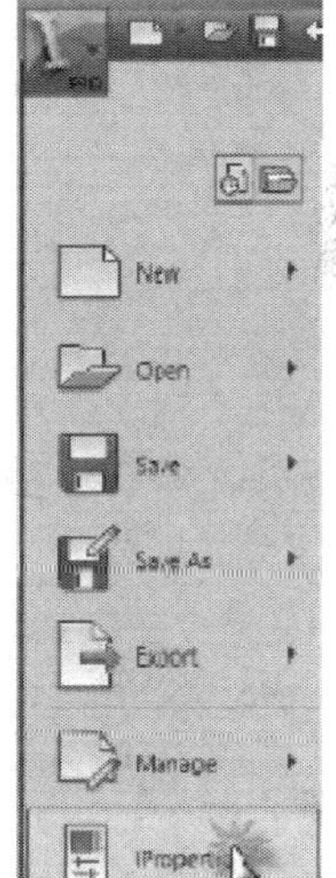

The choice returns this dialog box:

Choose the tab **Summary**

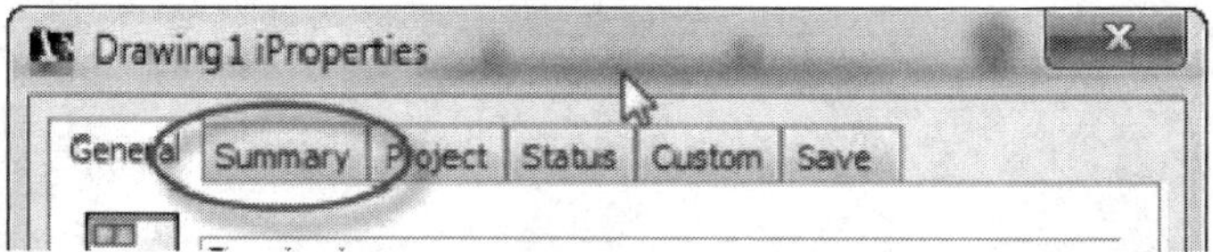

Dialog boxes refer to the fields provided:

Enter the appropriate information in fields

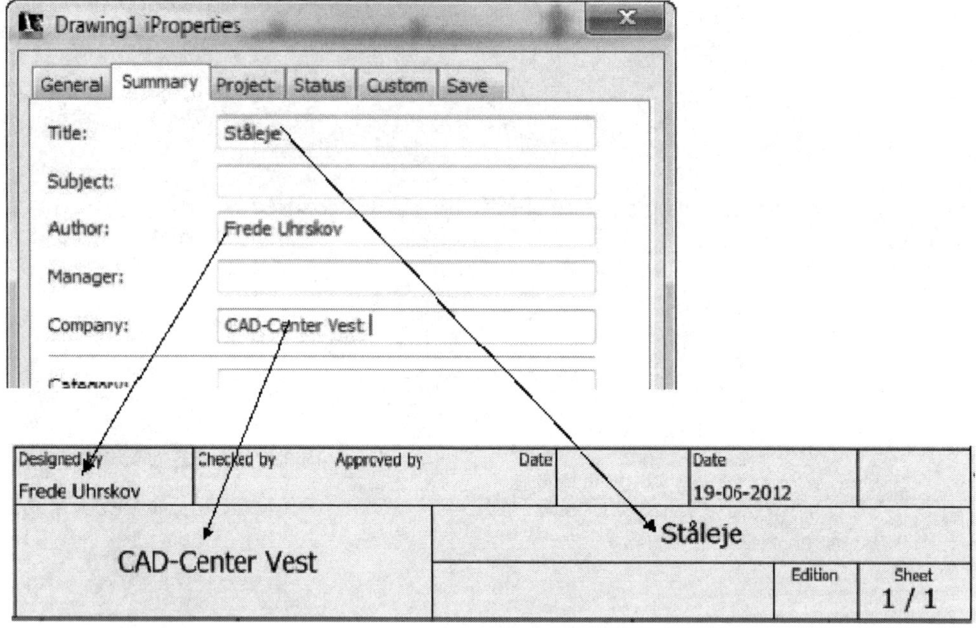

Choose the tab **Project**

This tab is in this case not so important.

Creation of views

The various plots are controlled by the panel **Place Views**

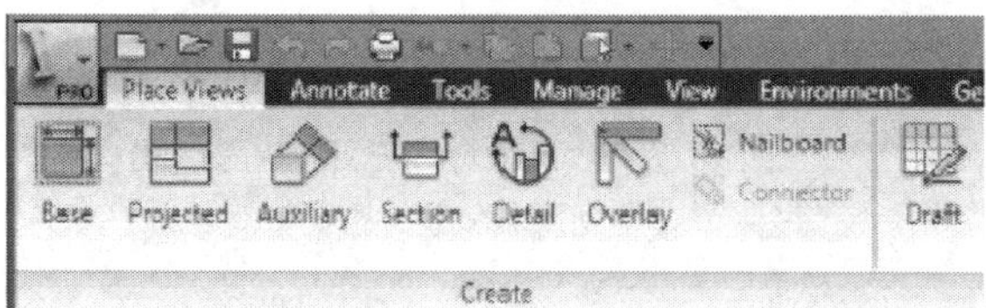

The first thing we do is create a **View** by clicking the field provided:

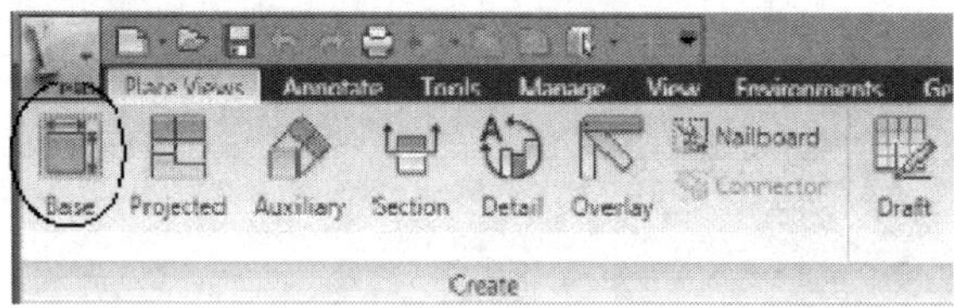

Up comes a dialog where we can see the current part the box **File.**

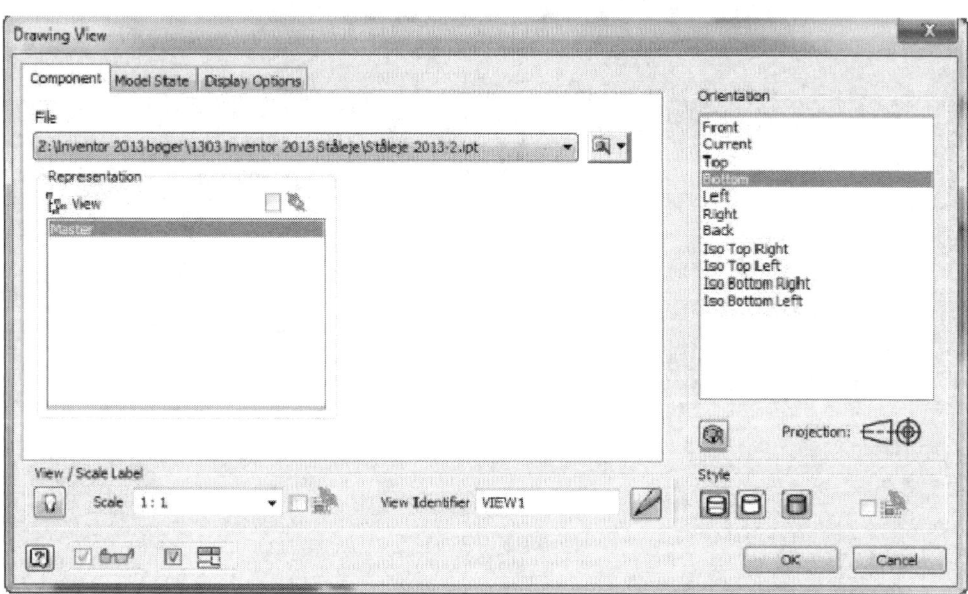

If there is no open part - you can browse the requested file:

When the file is found, you will see a model of party member in the paper.

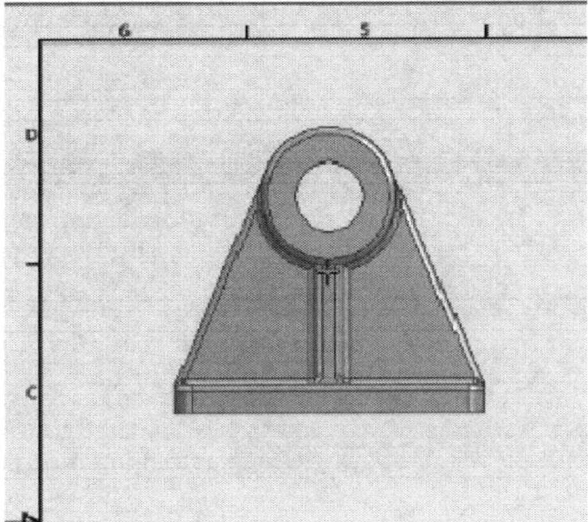

If the displayed representation is not satisfactory, you can change the image in this field:

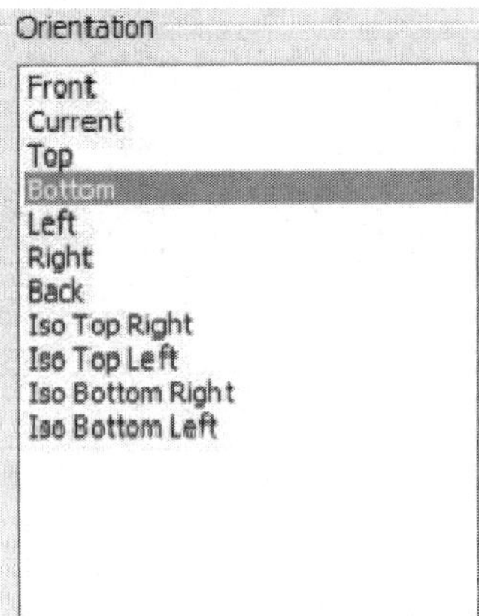

If there are some real options that meet your needs, you can define the desired **View** by clicking this button:

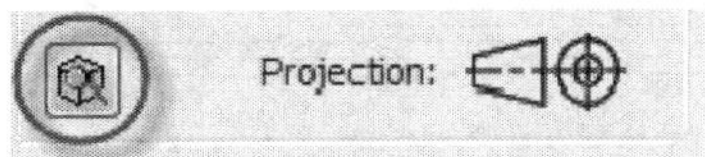

Now showing the desired level in the view:

Click to create the view. This can now be placed in the desired location on fre paper:

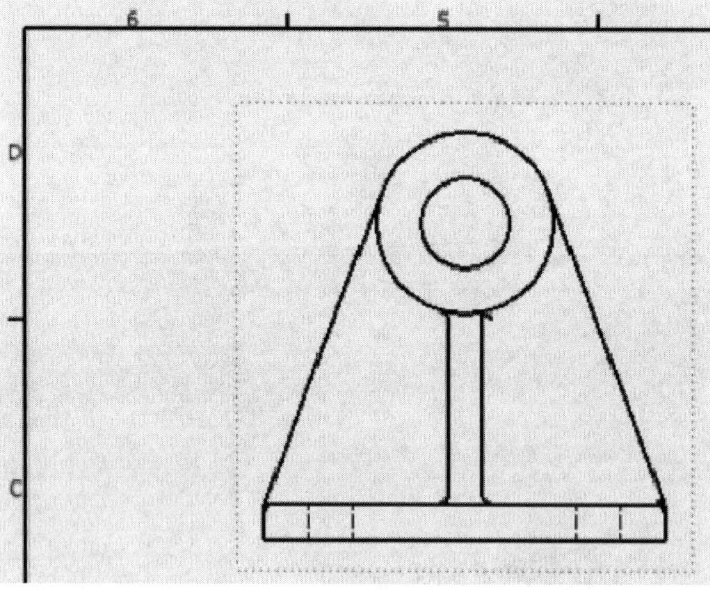

We must now create the other 2 designs - choose **Projected View** - only if you got out of the command.

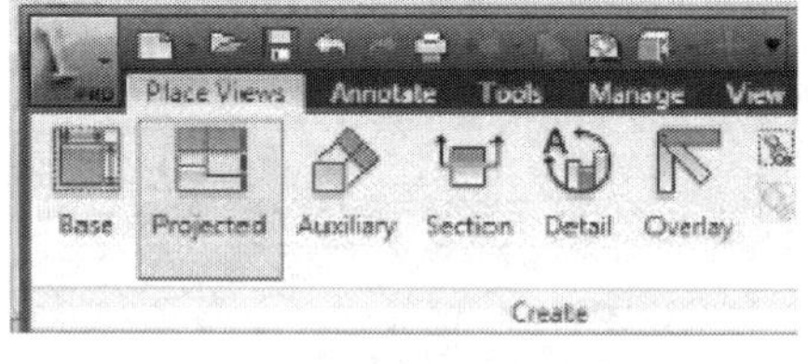

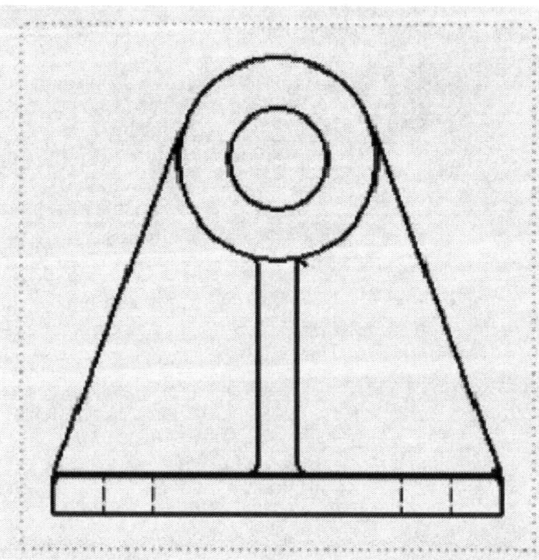

                    Copyright © 2012 Frede Uhrskov

Pull to the right - note that a projected model appears - Click on the place where you want the model located:

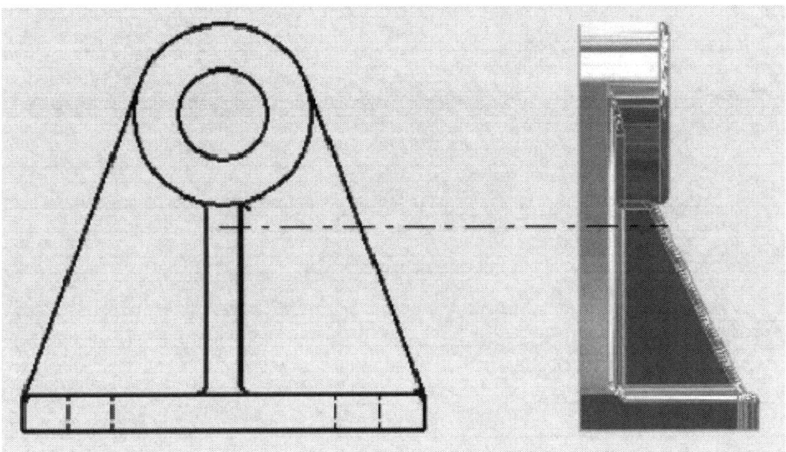

 Pull down - note that a projected model appears - Click on the place where you want the model located:

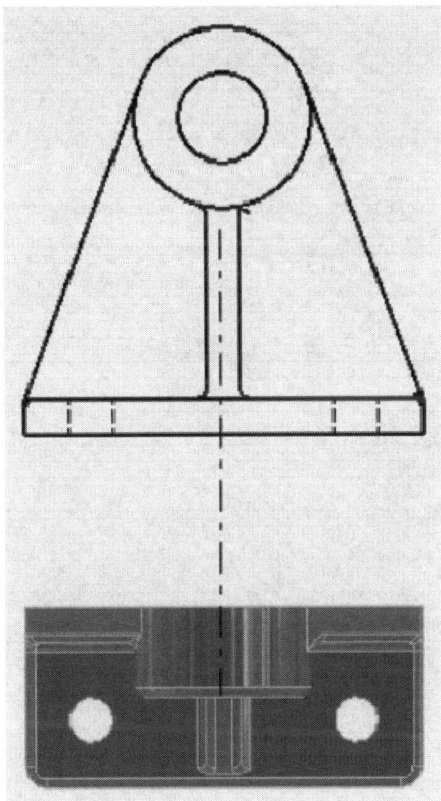

Drag diagonally downward to the right - note that an isometric model appears - Click on the place where you want the model located:

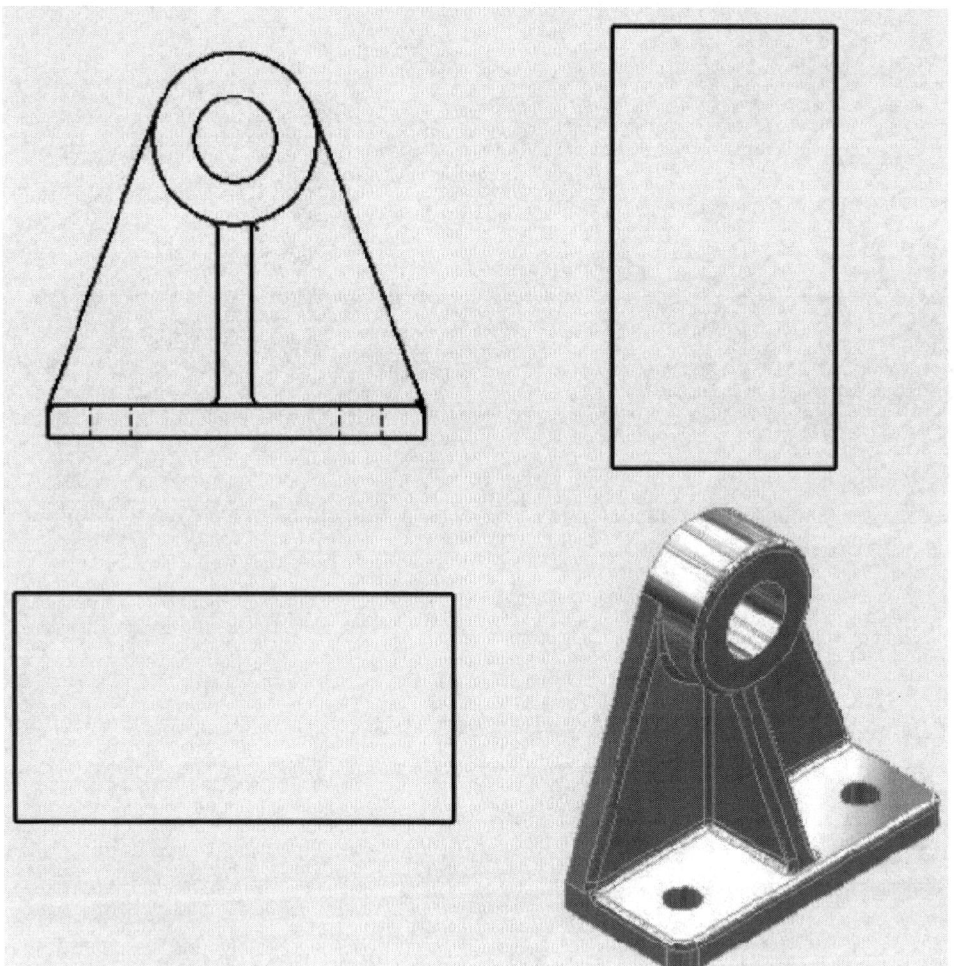

Notice that the first models are not generated yet - there are only empty squares.

Right Click and Choose **Create:**

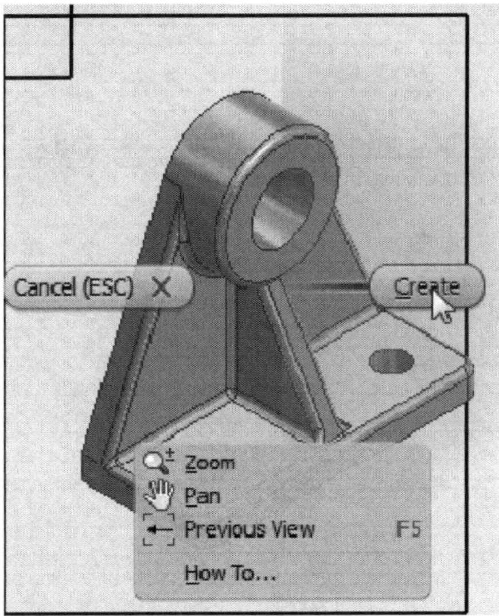

Now all the models are generated - including hidden lines:

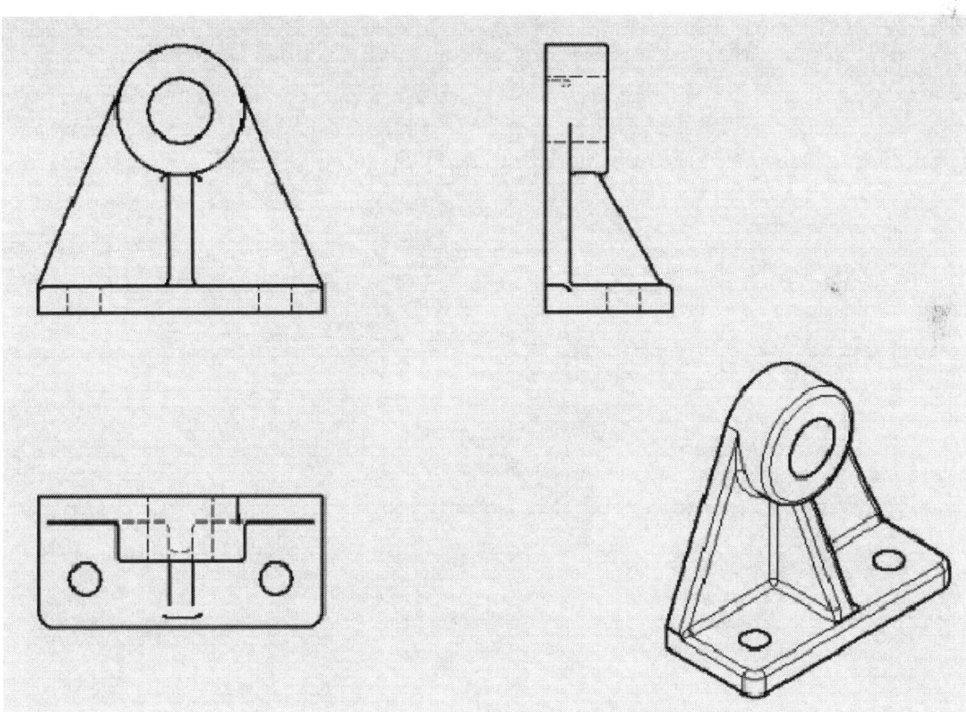

As seen, there are no dimensions in the models, and before we will put it onto the drawing. Before that we will change a little in the default setup **DIMSTYLE.**

Choose **Edit Layers**

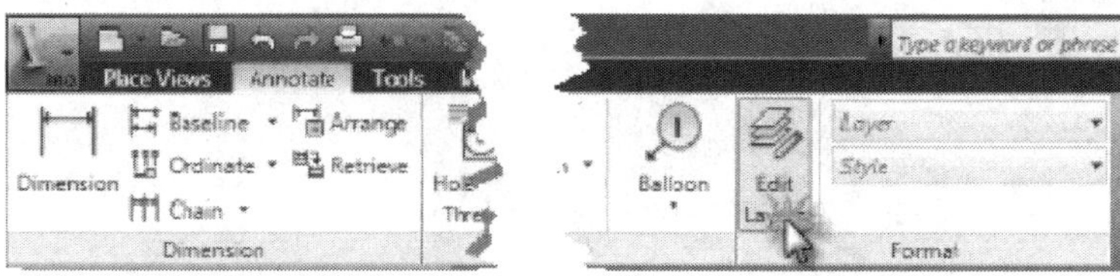

A dialog box comes up:

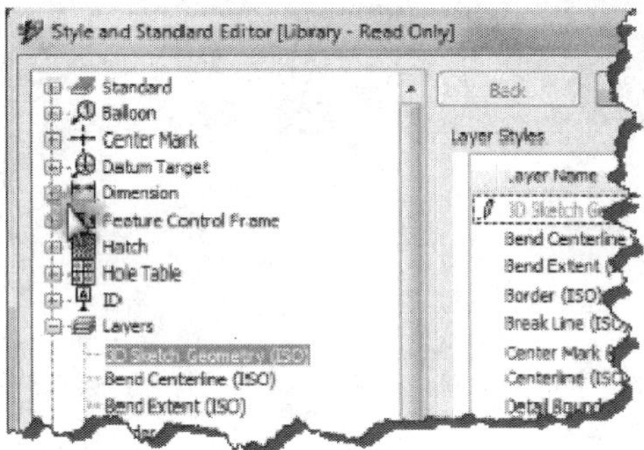

Click the plus sign next to **Dimensions** and then Click on the **Default ISO**

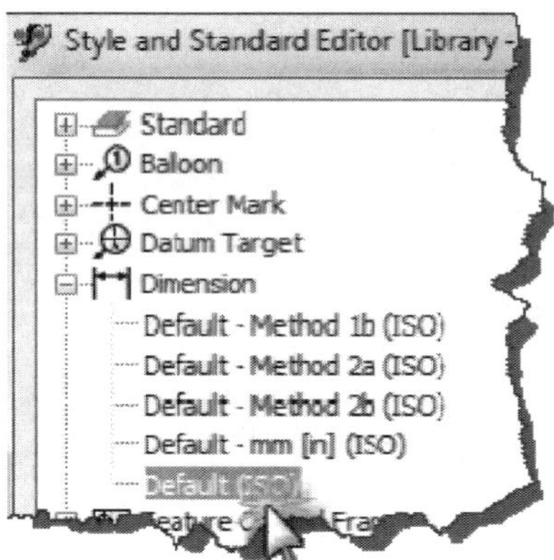

                                        Copyright © 2012 Frede Uhrskov

On the right side of the dialog box the predetermined settings for the DIMSTYLE are shown.

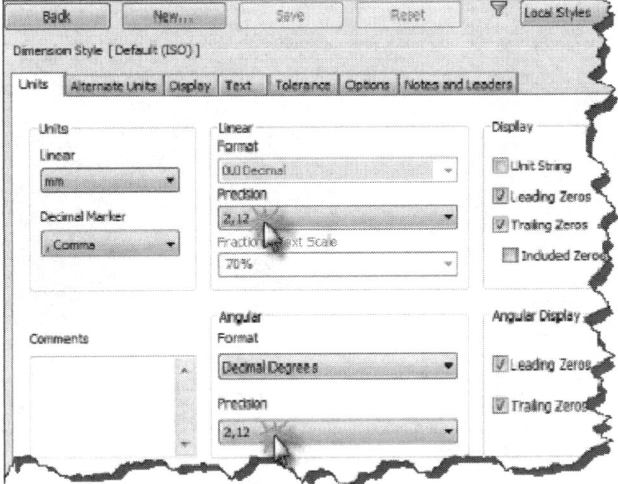

Make the indicated changes:

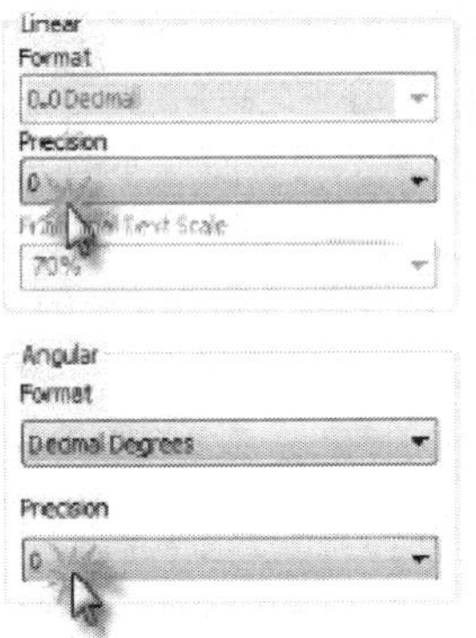

Click **Done**

To view the objective is relevant for each view, right click in the view and choose **Retrieve Dimensions ...**

Then a dialog box opens:

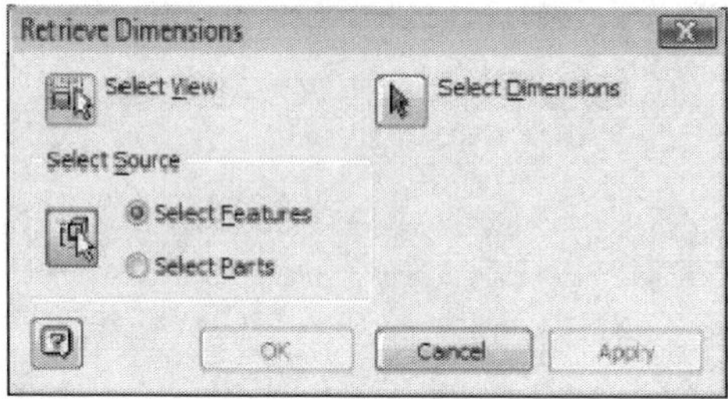

Choose **Select Parts** and then point to a party member in the selected view.

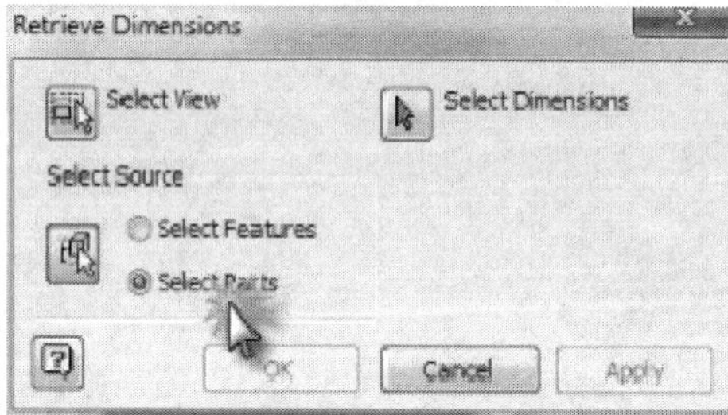

Copyright © 2012 Frede Uhrskov

Now choose the box **Select Dimensions,** then the relevant dimensions for that view is displayed - now drag a window around all dimensions, or name the dimensions that you want displayed.

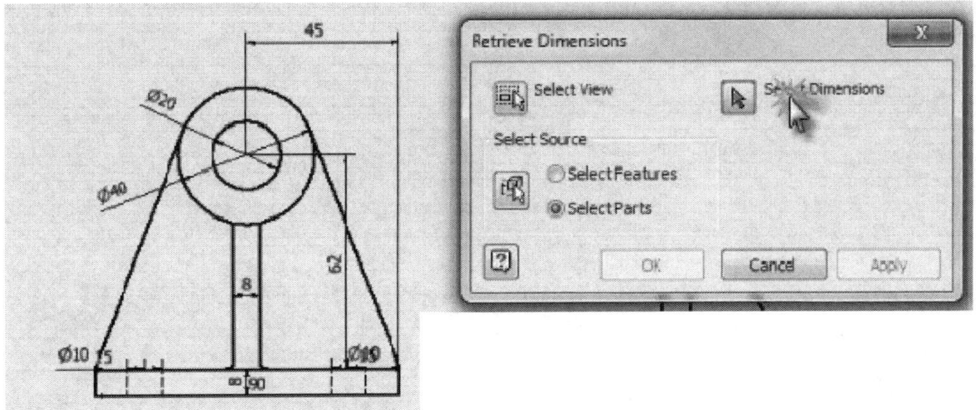

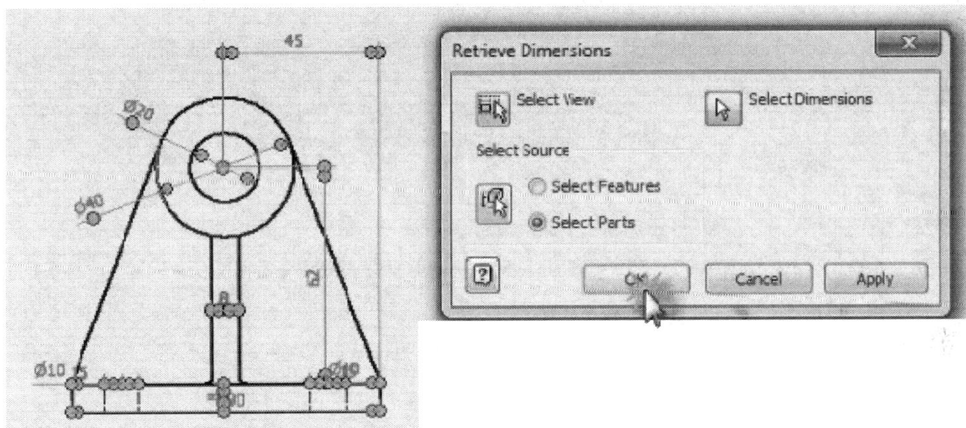

Click **Ok** - now dimensions are placed in the drawing. Repeat the same process in the other views.

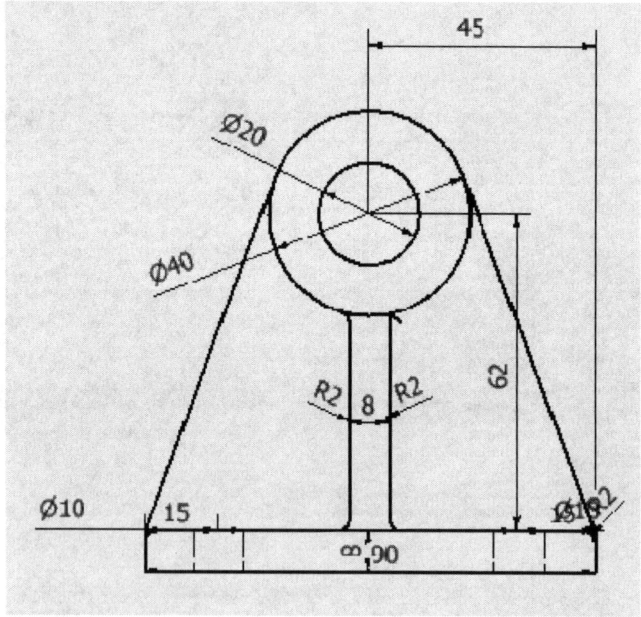

Dimension positions are changed by clicking on the object and hold the left mouse button - then move the dimension to the desired position.

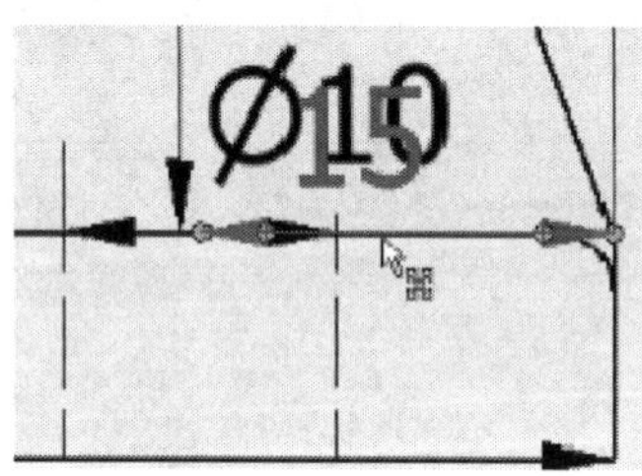

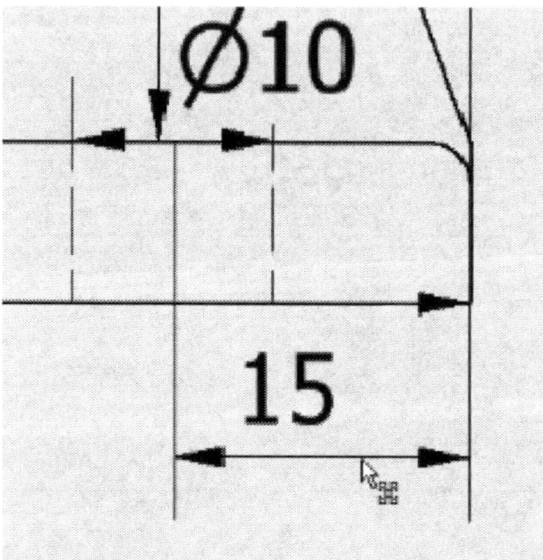

Section view

We will now make a section view in the bearing house.

Create a new drawing with template **Standard.idw**

Insert a **Base View** of bearing house

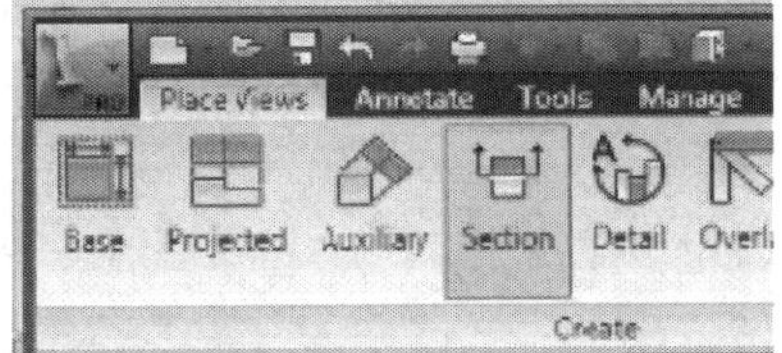

Choose **Section View**

Click on the view in which you want the section line made - Inventor snaps automatically to the appropriate places in the topic - snap to the center of the circle - without Click and drag the cursor outside of the topic:

Click where you want the section line to start.

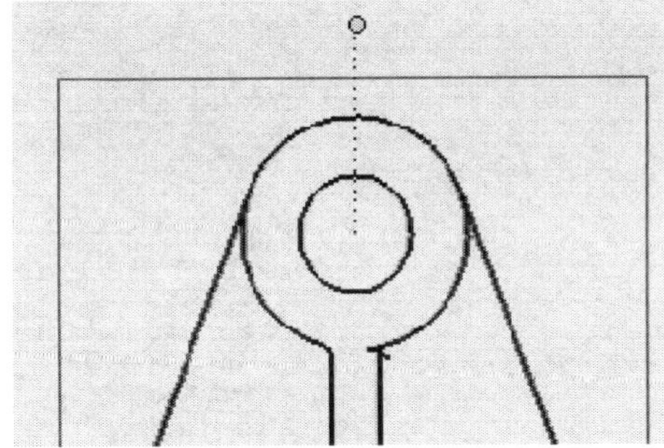

Now pull the section line through the subject:

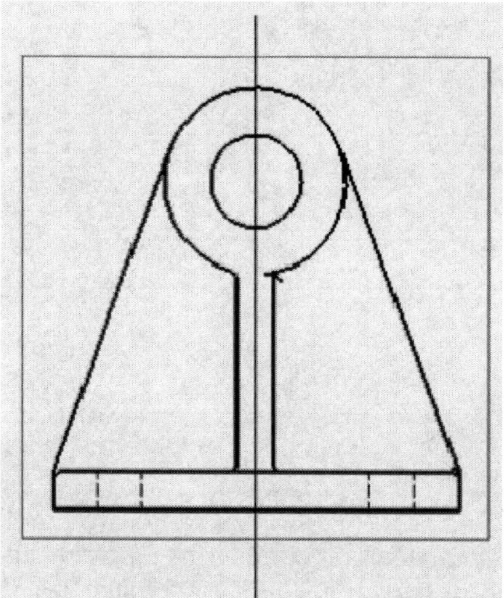

When you click at the end point of the section line, right click and choose **Continue**

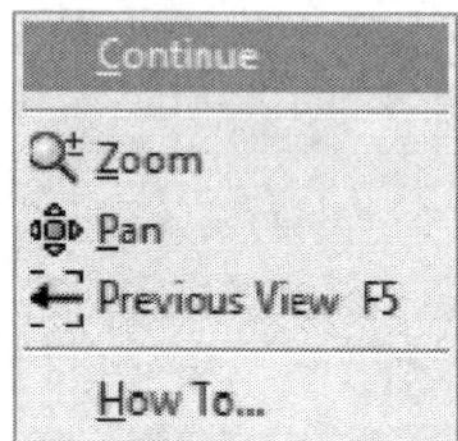

Then a dialogue box appears in which you can write section names:

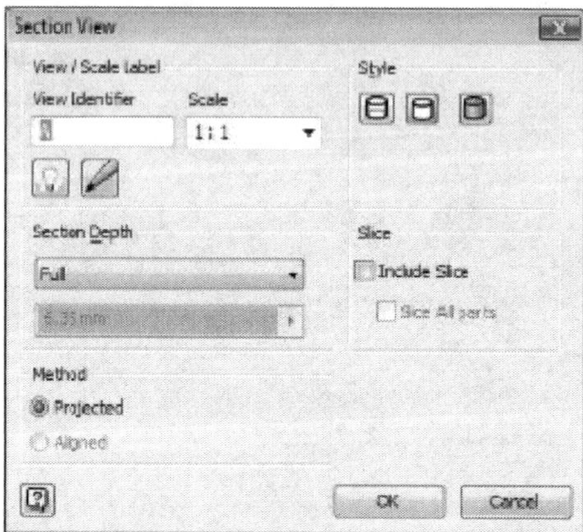

Simultaneously with the appearance of the dialog box, drag the section to the desired location:

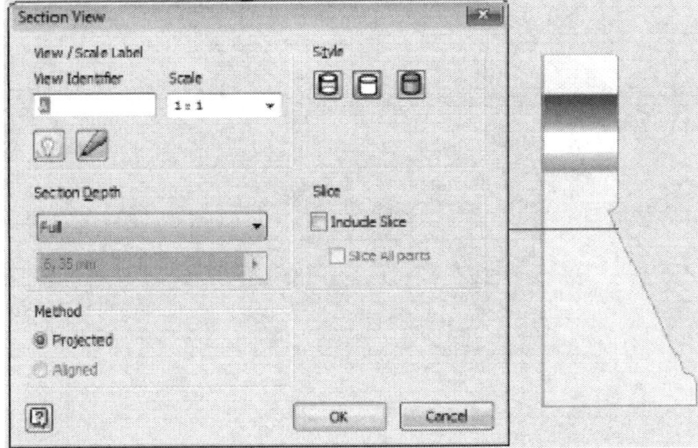

Click where you want the section placed and click **OK** in the dialog box - now the section is generated.

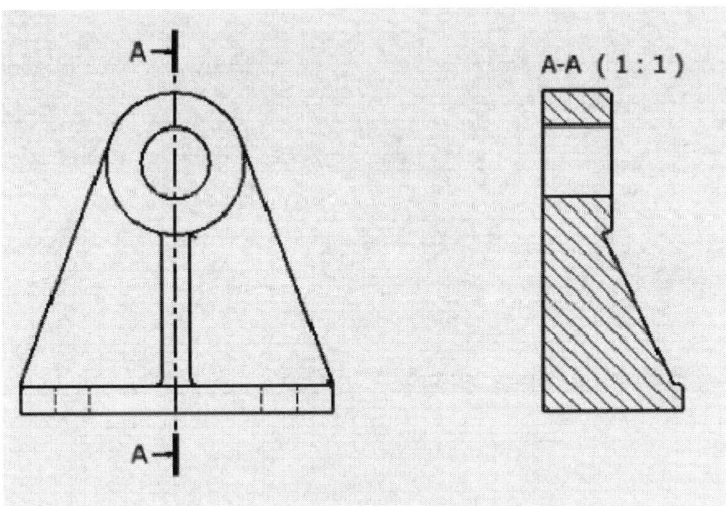

Now create in a similar manner a section in the displayed view - note that you can place the section perpendicular to the interview - we will correct later:

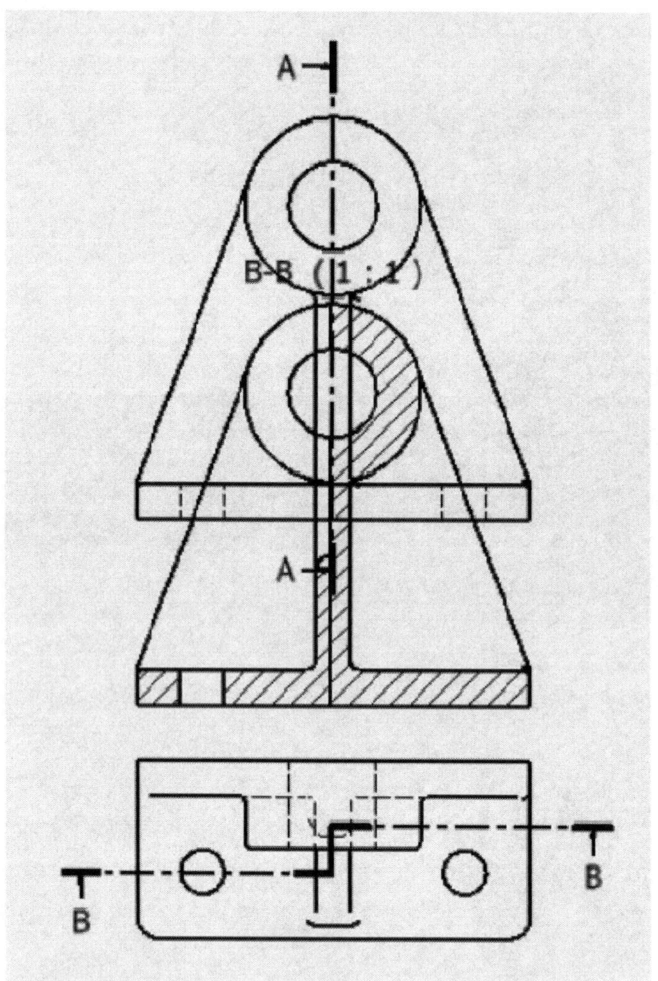

Right Click the new sections and choose **Alignment -> Break**

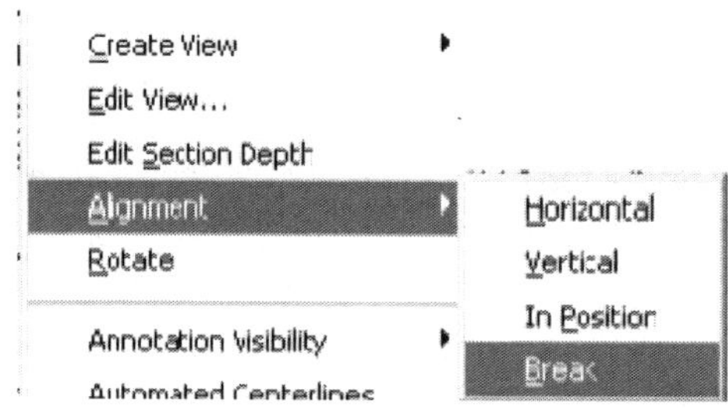

Now, the section is placed where you want it:

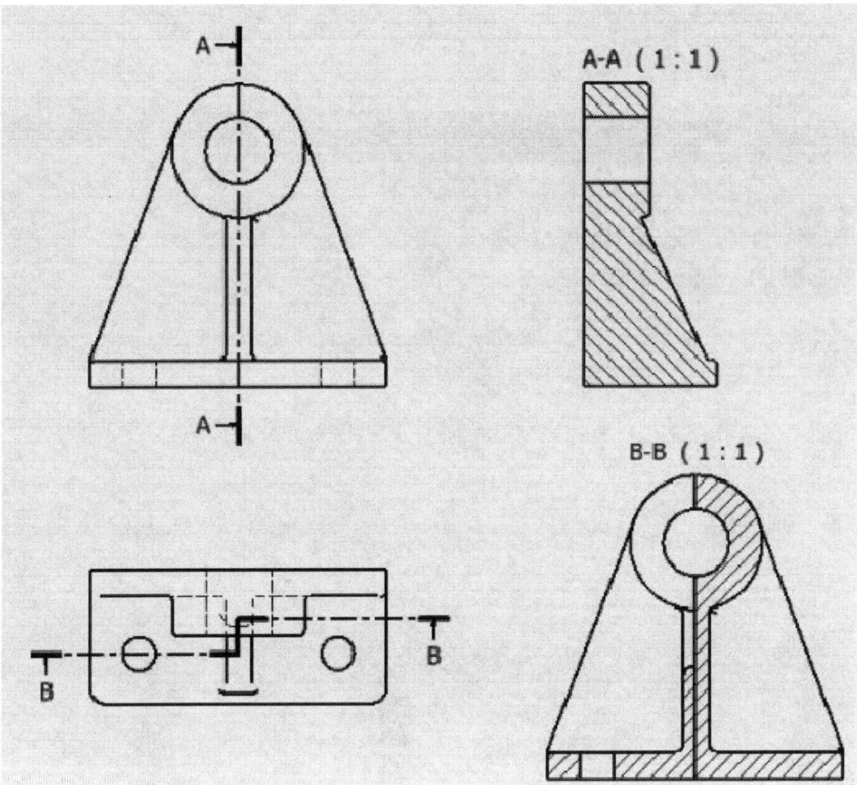

Line Width

Setting up the line widths are controlled by a dialog box which is retrieved by the **Format -> Styles Editor**

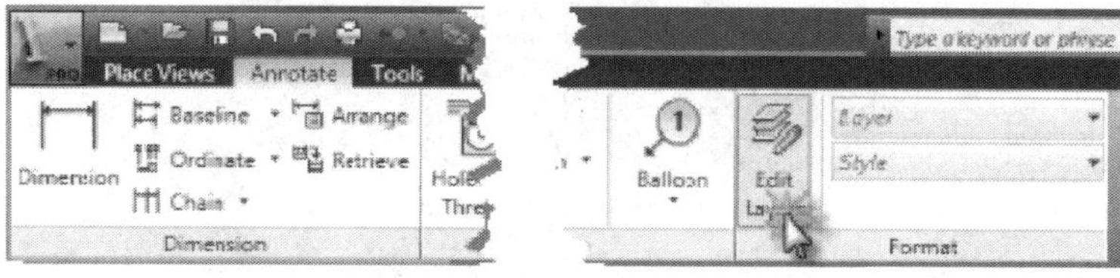

In the dialog box choose **Layer.** This displays all line types - especially the section line thickness seems somewhat excessive.

Choose therefore **Section Line** and Click on the figure for line width - now displays a drop down. These are standard widths.

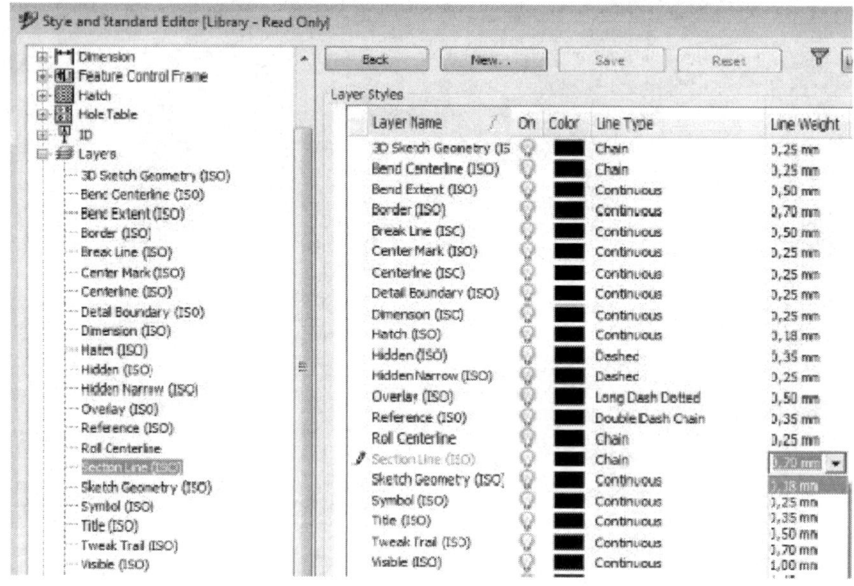

Right Click and **Update Style**

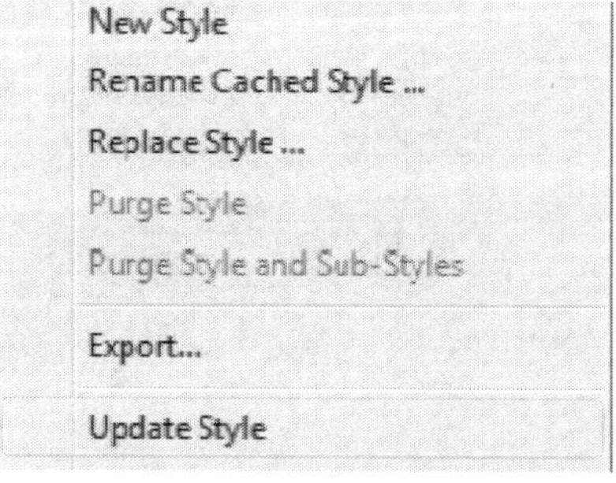

After changing the line width of the section line drawing could possibly look like this:

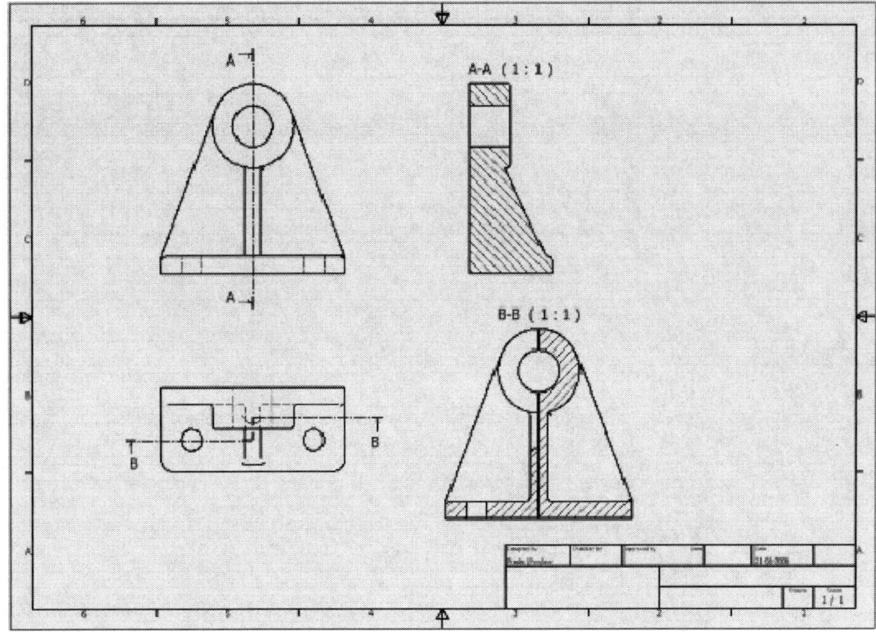